The Winter Repertory
Michael Feingold / General Editor

WR1   Kenneth Bernard *Night Club and Other Plays*

WR2   María Irene Fornés *Promenade and Other Plays*

WR3   Tom Eyen *Sarah B. Divine! and Other Plays*

WR4   Sam Shepard *Mad Dog Blues and Other Plays*

WR5   Robert Patrick's *Cheep Theatricks!*

WR6   Rochelle Owens, ed. *Spontaneous Combustion: Eight New American Plays*

WR7   Stanislaw Ignacy Witkiewicz *Tropical Madness: Four Plays*

A Winter Repertory Special Edition:

Jacobs and Casey *Grease:*
The New '50s Rock Musical

12345678 12345678 12345678 12345678

the
winter repertory

Spontaneous Combustion
Eight
New American Plays

EDITOR: ROCHELLE OWENS

WINTER HOUSE LTD

NEW YORK

The editor wishes to thank, for various kindnesses, Elisabeth Marton, Michael Feingold, and George Economou.

Photo credits: Photo of Adrienne Kennedy courtesy of *Vogue,* Copyright © by The Condé Nast Publications, Inc. Photo of Julie Bovasso by Walt Burton; of Ed Bullins, by Doug Harris; of William M. Hoffman, by Andy Milligan; of Megan Terry, by Bert Andrews.

To the memory of
Yetta Adler and Trisevgeni Economou:
the grandmothers

Introduction
Rochelle Owens
page 1

Sun
Adrienne Kennedy   3

Cinque
Leonard Melfi   15

Dialect Determinism
Ed Bullins   55

Sanibel and Captiva
Megan Terry   71

A Quick Nut Bread to Make Your Mouth Water
William M. Hoffman   105

Schubert's Last Serenade
Julie Bovasso   149

Ba-Ra-Ka
Imamu Amiri Baraka (LeRoi Jones)   175

He Wants Shih
Rochelle Owens   183

INTRODUCTION

I know a biologist who is not chicken-hearted, who is a sensible and calm man, and he says that the human race has only thirty years left on this planet—and that's that. It seems the atmospheric belt around our old globe is boiling, curdling and mixing with all the industrial gaseous noxiousness civilization can concoct. (Why do we let mush-heads fold up and stomp down our universe like it was an empty beer can?!) Living in this technological age, as overwhelming to us as the Age of the Ungorgeous Dinosaur was to our prehistoric ancestors, we carry around with us a diabolical knowledge—and a terrible blood-chilling indifference to the blistering that is the end result of that knowledge. Even the paper we mark our histories on is a technological miracle and a part of the scientific horror—the books that make eternal the memory of a human's inspiration are ghastly skinny slices of excessively mashed wood—don't laugh!

The substance we sling our imagery onto, part and parcel of the technological madness we tolerate, is one of the psychic links between the eight of us, something we share as playwrights, along with the knowledge of bloodlettings and anguish, and a commitment to define that ambiguous eleventh commandment. All of us stand on this maddening and dangerous American earth, bearing witness to the everlasting meaningfulness of the external world our country is depredating. Eight of us, female and male, white and black, with diverse political and esthetic needs, refusing to abide by lists of rules and definitions of how to make plays "come across" and "communicate with the audience." We won't be decorative playwrights, laying on falseness over the false emotional structures of false people: Authentic theater oscillates between joyousness and fiendishness. It needs the lucidity of maniacs, and their passionate innocence. We are logicians; we are contrary people. We want to ease the human soul's tension. We write for the sake of your spirit, not afraid of the menacing half-human gadgets with shoes who would affix us to a wall and make us bow with their useless rules when they pull the chain. We are mystics; we are contrary people. We hate human oppression, especially our own. (O especially our own!)

Three and a half billion people on earth by the year 2000.
American cheerleaders twirl white hard-rubber toy guns. There are
sanctimonious kids who want the hated parents to die. They also
want world peace. Three and a half billion people. And we warn you
to stand clear of the fatted calf. We must all stop the gluttony! For
us it is not enough that you should evolve into a musical-comedy-
lover-interpersonal-psychological-feeler-upper of domestic relations.
We write for the sake of your spirit. The playwright as creator or
incredible illuminated sea sponge absorbs the living present and then
lets it stream forth in mysterious electric rays. We have spirit and
optimistic hearts and we are convinced. (Once upon a time there
were two maniacs in Salonika!) We believe in the human race as a
living phenomenon that will not just rot and die. But—three and a
half billion people.

In Pakistan they throw lime over rotting corpses so that the
smell will be covered up. But suppose the corpse stood up and threw
off the lime and a spot of light and shadow moved on the violent
forms of the corpse. And it said, "I love language, don't sever me
from life. I want to play a role!"

    & that grand celestial
gargantuan voice said:
    "Lowly man &
Woman do not recognize
    thyself
      anymore!
THOU HAST SEEN ENOUGH."

Rochelle Owens
New York City

SUN
Adrienne Kennedy

A poem inspired by the death of Malcolm X

For my father, C.W. Hawkins

Sun is a poem-play permeated with revelations and magical
symbolism. Like an artist of the Middle Ages, Adrienne
Kennedy constructs a world of pain and terror; a human
being, cruelly shattered, whirls in a miasma of cosmic
forms. In this image, so intense in its compassion, the
writer has somehow concentrated both the murderous facts
of our time and the endlessly repeated history of our dreams.

NOTE: MOVEMENTS

Movements of the Man
His orbiting
Sun's orbiting
Movements of the Moon
Movements of the Sun
Wire
Revolving of the head

MAN   Flowers and Water

Steel wire appears encircling them.

The adoration of kings and a
kneeling youth

Red flashes.

A madonna and a child, a man
a madonna and a child and a
unicorn a study of a kneeling angel

Red sun flashes top left. Moon image moves. MAN *watches the*
red sun, tries to move his arms upward toward it.

there exist landscapes flowers
and water views of the coast of
Italy cloudbursts lilies a
mountain a mountain of lilies

A purple light. MAN *tries to move his arms.*

and the heart,

Red sun revolves. HE *watches it and tries to move. A yellow light.*
Half of the Moon vanishes. HE *watches it fearfully over his*

shoulder as the half slowly drifts away. Then before him HE
watches red sun revolving. It disappears in front of him, lower
left. MAN *is still, then looks again at vanished half moon.*

Yes, and the heart and the tendrons
of the neck a landscape with a
view over a valley mountains
beyond a drawing of a square castle

Orange sun appears top right.
Greater hope.

Yes, my heart and tendrons
of the neck landscapes mountains
a drawing of a square castle

Moon still in half. Orange sun spins. MAN *watches greatly fearful*
as if the spinning sun held a grim omen, but goes on speaking
hopefully.

the head of a man, yes a man's
head a man's shoulders the
organs of a woman an embryo
in the uterus the heart a
nude man a nude man
with his arms stretched out

Pause. Intently watches orange sun spin.

As a young man I felt myself
to be in the midst of sun

Orange sun spins. Yellow sun now appears, spins. Beautiful
sound. Could be this spinning.

I liked to think my heart
led to light. Yet I discerned
coming dishonor.

*Sound and yellow and orange suns vanish. As always, when
things vanish, MAN is greatly perturbed. A black sun flashes top
center then goes downward. HE watches its downward descent.
Silence. Behind him the moon loses a quarter. HE watches it over
his shoulder. The quarter vanishes slowly, moving away from
him.*

Yes the position of my blood vessels
the blood vessels in my face
a nude man with his arms
stretched out my lungs my
main arteries. *(Pause)*
a branch of blackberry

*Black sun that has remained grows larger, a purple light. MAN
watches black sun grow large.*

Yes, water in motion a
spray of a plant a domed
church, a flying machine
horses horses and riders

*A yellow sun flashes orbits the wire vanishes. Moon still at quarter.
Now at lower right the MAN's disembodied head appears. Large
black sun vanishes wire starts to move slowly in a circle. Long
silence. MAN speaks looking at dismembered head before him.*

My head, the head of Christ
the head of an apostle head
of St. Anne Head of the Virgin
Head of the infant St. John
Head of the infant Jesus. *(Pause)*
my head dismembered

Staring at his dismembered head disbelieving.

No, I still dream children
children, the body and arms

of a child. *(Pause)*
Yet my head. Dead

HE *goes on staring at his head as a black sun orbits twice. New light comes onto the whole scene. Full moon comes again, but a slightly different texture, more disturbing. Wire still slowly moving.* MAN *waits. The position of the moon,* MAN, *wire, head and all slightly change position so now less symmetry exists. The expression on the face of the head changes. All of these changes seem to be felt within the* MAN *since they are his inner state. The* MAN *'s own head grows distorted as* HE *watches the wire move around him. His head watches him, comes closer, smiles. Wire closer. Then a long waiting. Great imbalance of objects. Then loudly the moon fragments slowly and completely to pieces. Long fragmentation.* HE *tries to watch from his angular position.* HE *waits. Long fragmentation. Red sun appears top right. As the moon loudly totally fragments behind him* HE *looks up at the new red sun.*

When a new sun appears
I think before I was born
my mother dreamed she saw
me in the sun then the
sun went down and at
night I appear within
the moon . . . And as the moon
fragments and all is imbalanced
I keep on thinking landscapes
flowers and water views
of the coast of Italy
cloudbursts lilies, a
mountain of lilies the heart

Moon fragments again. Red sun revolves closer to MAN *'s face. Orange sun appears, drops across him, disappears. Head watches* MAN *as* MAN *watches all. Fragmented moon, red sun, vanished orange sun.*

Yet all is in imbalance
no I must think of
trees, a tree, a tree
no a tree, a tree.
Water in motion

Red sun revolves rapidly, closer to his own face and starts to spin
mysteriously, before his face.

No rocks and streams
and flowers and violas
and sketches of landscapes
a river with a canal
alongside and a castle
on a hill flower rushes

His dismembered head vanishes.

star of Bethlehem
and other plants . . .
a spray of brambles

Sun passes through his face leaving a light before him. Loud noise
of the moon fragmenting on his ear.

No rocks and streams
and flowers and violas
and sketches of landscapes
a river with a canal
alongside and a castle
on a hill

Louder fragmenting.

flowering rushes, a star
of Bethlehem and other
plants . . . a spray of brambles

A smell of a spray of brambles fills the air. MAN *'s arms appear more disjointed.* MAN *continues loudly fragmenting, an orange spinning sun .appears lower left dismembered head appears top left and starts to orbit wire still revolving slowly a disembodied arm appears lower right.*

the sun is now myself
dismembered in darkness
my blood my dismembered
self at sundown on the moon.

HE *watches his arm. The sun slowly vanishes moving upward beyond his vision.* HE *understands that his own arms are growing more disjointed. Noises of spattering. Suddenly blood starts to run out of the fragmented moon. Smell of blood.* MAN *grows more disjointed while his head orbits and while blood runs out of the dark fragmented moon. Great smell of blood, noises of spattering as if the blood were falling against his head.*

No the head of this man
a man's head and shoulders
the organs of my woman
as embryo in the uterus
its heart
this nude man
this nude man with his
arms stretched out

HE *tries to stretch his arms. Suddenly many suns explode over the* MAN. *More blood pours out of the fragmented moon. More suns explode. Wire revolves closer to his head. His dismembered head. Still orbiting. A disembodied leg appears, vanishes. In the third time suns explode over the whole scene very slowly blood stops pouring out of the fragmented moon. Very slowly suns stop exploding and very slowly the fragmented moon changes into the* MAN *very slowly limb by limb the limbs slightly bloodied. Very slowly. At the same time his head silently revolves and at the same time very slowly blood comes onto his own face and* HE

becomes blotted out by it. HE *lowers his blotted head. Silence.*
Head revolves. His own head blotted blank by blood.

When I was young I did
dream myself to be in the
midst of suns now fragmented
in the moon I am the head
of a bear the paws of a
dog the paws of a wolf
heads of monsters, a dragon . . .
a lizard symbolizing this truth
Now where is my head the
head of Christ the head of
an apostle head of St. Anne
Head of the Virgin head of
the infant St. John, head
of the infant Jesus. Where?

Silence. Revolving head stops. Orange spinning sun appears,
lower right. MAN, *now more disjointed, with blotted head.*

I still dream of a woman
wearing a bodice of interlaced
ribbons a young woman
the head of a girl a girl's
braided hair the human
figure in a circle, man
man carrying earth
As my head moves
dead as the bones
and tendrons of
my arm move dead I still dream
Still I dream of the heart

The whole scene starts moving into imbalance.

The position of the blood vessels
in the neck and the face

Dark blue and purple suns appear, revolve.

A crowned eagle standing on a globe

The moon, the MAN, *the wire the head all moving to a new imbalance. Then limb by limb the* MAN*'s body becomes blotted by blood.*

Yes the heart
the head and shoulders of a man
muscles of the face and arms
a nude man
organs of a woman
an embryo in the uterus
the heart
Tuscany
A tree

The MAN*'s body becomes more blotted by blood while the symmetry of the scene is lost. Disembodied legs appear then vanish.*

Arezzo
Borgho
San Sepulchro
Perugia
Chiusi and Siena

The whole scene moves violently. The boundaries of the moon vanish. Black suns revolve. In the moon MAN*'s body falls apart.*

Two trees on the
bank of a stream
I still dream

His body in the moon falls apart as the moon totally loses boundaries and all parts of his body fly into space.

A river with a rope ferry.

Wire breaks. Flashing grey and black suns. Collision of objects. Great collision, then the MAN *who is blotted out by blood becomes smaller and smaller. Great collision of his flying limbs.* HE *becomes smaller and smaller and vanishes into a tiny red sun.*

Vanished MAN*'s voice:*

The Arno

MAN *has vanished into a tiny red sun. Red sun turns black.*

Vanished MAN*'s voice:*

A river with a canal alongside

Flying limbs become still, vanish. Wire vanishes. All vanishes except tiny black sun.

Vanished MAN*'s voice:*

and a castle on a hill
flowering rushes.
I still

Darkness.

CINQUE
Leonard Melfi

For Ellen Stewart

Cinque is filled with the heartbroken, funny and freaky characters Leonard Melfi draws from America's best mythology—the cartoon. A group of fabulous Western caricatures drifts together and spins off into an eccentric and madly playful adventure of love and illusion, all the while smoking their heads off with cigarettes—a unique perception of the American comi-tragedy: deep and unfulfilled desires crossed up by a powerful drive toward self-destruction.

THE PEOPLE OF THE PLAY, as they appear:

SHERIFF SUNSHINE: His age is about thirty and his hair is blond-brown with lots of waves and scattered curls and it reaches down to his broad shoulders; and he wears a white shirt and he also wears a pair of tight-fitting white trousers; the neck line of his shirt bears a bright red stripe and so do the ankle lines of his trousers; on the front of his beaming white shirt there is a huge bright circle of glowing red, perfectly formed, resembling the bull's eye of a target, and the bright red circle is surrounded by a close thin white circle, which is then surrounded by a close thin khaki circle, which is then finally surrounded by an even thinner circle of straight black: in the center of the bright red circle there are a few smears of more straight black; on the back of his beaming white shirt there is the same identical design; he wears dark brown cowboy boots beautifully spit-shined, with blinding silver spurs; he wears a rich black leather belt-holster which holds two brand new silver pistols; he also wears a large cowboy hat made of deep smooth black felt; and finally once more: he is sporting the gleaming badge of the sheriff.

TOM BROWN: His age is more like nineteen or twenty and his hair is very straw-colored and soon it will be just as long as the sheriff's hair; and he wears a crisp white shirt with greyish-blue scribbling about the collar; his trousers are a light golden color; a vague dark golden image/impression of some sort of past animal spreads about the areas of his trousers and up into the whiteness of his shirt; he wears a light golden belt-holster that holds a single light golden pistol; he also wears a pair of dark golden cowboy boots and spurs that match his belt-holster and pistol; his nice neat large cowboy hat is bright white.

MAUDE SMITH: Her age is anywhere between forty and fifty (it's hard to tell because she always looks pretty good) and she is the mother of Tom Brown; her dyed brown hair (it's almost spar-kling dark red) always has a permanent wave; she is all dressed up in an immaculate white dress that goes to the floor and billows out everywhere after it leaves her waist; the white dress is patterned with deep green rectangles that are framed first by thin white, then with thin gold; there are incoherent white capital letters scratched into the center of the green rectangles; she wears a rather fancy belt of interwoven green material; finally: she wears a huge bourbon-colored bonnet.

HORACE WHITE: He is in his late forties and he looks very strong and very solid; his hair is a lot shorter than the hair of the other two men and it is sort of greying at the temples now; his shirt and trousers are white but there is a gold circle that runs about his neck line and his ankle line as well; on the front of his shirt and on the back of his shirt there is a royal blue symbol suggesting the abstract wings of a direct bird in direct flight which is trimmed at the top by a thin layer of gold and with a blue oval dot hovering erectly above it all; he wears a blue printed belt-holster that holds a blue pistol and it usually hangs lazily behind him; his mammoth cowboy hat is leather green, and his cowboy boots are leather black with silver spurs.

ABIGAIL PEPPER: She is approximately eighteen and her hair is long and lovely and the color of luscious lemons; she wears a long flowing one-piece gownlike dress that blooms below her waist like a precious parasol; the top part of the dress is mainly radiant red and the bottom part is basically willowy white; a design of white cuts into the breast section forming an exact center angle, and she wears a beltlike thing made of interwoven gold; at the ankle line of the dress there is a smattering of obvious black smudges that seem to add to the whole costume in a somewhat valid way; finally: she wears a bright light baby-blue-colored bonnet.

WHERE THEY ARE: Las Vegas, Nevada, America

WHEN: A whole night during 1969

Before the house lights go down and before the curtain goes up we hear the sweet semi-somber strumming of a lone guitar which is coming out with the sad-happy and the soft-solid sounds of a lazy lonesome light lime melody that is most likely being strummed away by a lazy lonesome cowboy or maybe even a lazy lonesome cowgirl: both full of living laxity. No matter: it all sounds very lovely . . . and special. But when the house lights decide to go down: things swiftly change: the quiet music transforms into something else: we hear a voice over the loudspeaker in the theatre; the voice reminds us of a politician we might have heard many times before; or perhaps: one of those bygone radio announcers who used to be MC's on all those various radio programs after eleven-thirty at night from all those various night clubs of all those various hotels from all over America during the forties and the early fifties.

THE VOICE   *(In the darkness)* It affords me great joy to have him on this program, and to present to you for the final band of the night: one of the most popular bands in the United States at the moment: Mr. Glenn Miller.

We hear fond and loving applause coming from the loudspeaker; and then we hear the Glenn Miller Orchestra playing its theme song: "Moonlight Serenade."

As the music plays, the curtain slowly rises. We see a vast cyclorama that rambles in a gigantic half-circle from the left of the stage to the right of the stage. The yellow lights, warm and comforting, begin to come up on the cyclorama: revealing a soft smooth sprawling watercolor that tells us we are in a very romantic-image version-vision of Las Vegas. We also see a staggered line of five various-sized merry-go-round-colored-looking rocking horses facing the audience, and they are all rocking by themselves without rocking riders, and in slow and sentimental time with the music, and they look like big toys waiting for big people.

SHERIFF SUNSHINE *enters from our right, and as he does: the "Moonlight Serenade" theme stops. Another selection begins to play over the loudspeaker. It is as though someone has been dropping quarters into a jukebox somewhere. And possibly it would be very right if the second selection might be something like The Nitty Gritty Dirt Band's rendition of "Hard Hearted Hannah."*

SHERIFF SUNSHINE *stands there with a cigarette dangling from his mouth and* HE *puffs on it a whole lot: making lots of uncalled-for smoke;* HE *blows a few beautiful smoke rings too. Now* HE *begins to half-dance in relation to the blaring music.* HE *is very good at it.* HE *half-dances to the rocking horse that is situated in the center of the stage. It is the biggest horse of them all, and it is brightly painted the exact same colors as* SHERIFF SUNSHINE*'s costume color scheme.*

The rocking horses are all rocking a different pace now: it is the fast swinging rocking funky pace of the music that is playing now.

SHERIFF SUNSHINE *climbs onto his rocking horse, full-saddle, facing the audience, and then* HE *begins to rock with the music, a smoking cigarette always dangling from his mouth.*

TOM BROWN *enters from our left: also with a cigarette hanging from his mouth, smoking crazily.* HE *half-dances to his rocking horse painted to match his costume color scheme as well.* HE *straddles it fully, to the right of* SHERIFF SUNSHINE, *facing the audience, rocking away with his smoking cigarette hanging from his two lips.*

MAUDE SMITH *enters from a disguised opening in the center of the cyclorama, also with a lit cigarette hanging from her mouth.* SHE *dances fully to the music as* SHE *goes to her own color-schemed rocking horse: the last horse in the staggered line to our right.* SHE *climbs on the rocking horse: side-saddle, and begins to rock away too.*

The yellow lights are becoming deeper, better, and more beautiful. The vast cyclorama looks lovelier than ever. The music gets a little louder.

HORACE WHITE *enters from our right with a burning cigarette also dangling from his lips.* HE *half-dances to the music as* HE *moves to his rocking horse that is also painted to match the color scheme of his costume.* HE *climbs upon the horse, to the left of* SHERIFF SUNSHINE, *full-saddle, and rocks away too.*

And now it is time for the last entrance: it is ABIGAIL PEPPER, *and* SHE *comes happily through the disguised opening in the center of the cyclorama, also with a lit cigarette hanging from her mouth.* SHE *dances fully to the music as* SHE *heads toward her own color-schemed rocking horse which is the last horse in the staggered line to our left.* SHE *climbs on the rocking horse: side-saddle, and begins to rock away along with the rest of them.*

The glistening yellow-golden sunshine lights reach a fantastic shade of deep rich heights; and the music is way up now: as THEY *all rock away on their rocking horses, smoking, and facing the audience with great enjoyment.*

Finally: the music ends, and it is as though no more quarters have been dropped into the unseen jukebox. There is utter silence everywhere. Slowly: one-by-one: THEY *stop their individual rocking.* THEY *all look straight ahead and* THEY *all look somewhat puzzled. Instantly:* MAUDE SMITH *climbs off her rocking horse.* SHE *takes the cigarette from her mouth and crushes it out on the floor with her foot.* SHE *places her hands on her hips.*

MAUDE SMITH   What the hell's going on?!

ABIGAIL PEPPER *jumps off her rocking horse and holds her cigarette in her hand now.* SHE *screams and it is a parody of drama.*

ABIGAIL PEPPER   I've never been so depressed in my whole life! I've never been so unhappy in my whole life! *(*SHE *crushes her cigarette out on the floor with her foot)* In all my whole life: I've never been so depressed and so unhappy! *(*ABIGAIL PEPPER *exits through the disguised opening in the cyclorama.* SHE *is frantic and* SHE *is sobbing wildly)*

MAUDE SMITH   What the hell's going on?!

The minute ABIGAIL PEPPER *leaves there is a sudden bolt of lightning and a terrible crash of thunder. Everything becomes very dim for a second or two, and then everything returns to normal.* MAUDE SMITH *lights up another cigarette.*

I'm very nervous.

HORACE WHITE *suddenly jumps off his rocking horse.* HE *takes his cigarette out of his mouth and tosses it to the floor:* HE *crushes it with his foot.* HE *speaks, and it is desperate, and it is very much in the fashion that* ABIGAIL PEPPER *spoke upon her exit.*

HORACE WHITE   Sons-of-bitches and sons-of-bastards and sons-of-romance-killers too! *(*HORACE WHITE *exits wildly to our right)*

MAUDE SMITH   Wait a minute! Please, don't go . . . !

We hear the crazy roar of a crazy wind storm. It blows all over the stage: at their clothes: and the unoccupied rocking horses begin to rock by themselves now.

I'm getting *very* nervous. . . .

The wind storm begins to die out now. SHERIFF SUNSHINE *jumps off his rocking horse: but* HE *is very cool and easy and collected about it.* HE *crushes his cigarette out on the floor.*

SHERIFF SUNSHINE   Well: I'll be seein' you all. *(*SHERIFF SUNSHINE *lights up another cigarette)*

MAUDE SMITH   Are you going too . . . ?

SHERIFF SUNSHINE   See you around. *(*SHERIFF SUNSHINE *makes a slow sure exit to our right)*

MAUDE SMITH   Please, don't go. . . .

We hear the sweet semi-somber strumming that we heard before the house lights went down and the curtain went up.

What the hell's going on, Tom?!

TOM BROWN *starts to rock on his rocking horse again.*

TOM BROWN *(Cigarette still dangling from his mouth)* How do you like it, Mother Maude?

MAUDE SMITH How do I like what, Tom Brown?

TOM BROWN *begins to rock very fast on his rocking horse: it is as if he were a little boy at an improvised horse race.* HE *takes his cigarette from his mouth and tosses it to the floor while on top of his rocking horse.*

TOM BROWN My ranch house, Mother Maude.

MAUDE SMITH *goes and crushes his cigarette with her foot.*

MAUDE SMITH Oh, that. Well, I couldn't understand what you were saying the first time, Tom Brown. But it's a beautiful place. It's really a very beautiful place. I'm very proud of you, Tom Brown.

TOM BROWN *begins to rock and/or ride like a real live cowboy now: no kid stuff this time. The sweet semi-somber strumming continues to play on: it sounds very nice and relaxing.*

TOM BROWN It cost me a fortune.

MAUDE SMITH Oh, I can tell.

TOM BROWN But it's all right for me because I'm not married and I'm not a father and I'm making more money than I ever thought I would make.

MAUDE SMITH   But you've got to put some in the bank too, you know?

TOM BROWN   Oh, of course. I know that. For a windy day, right?

MAUDE SMITH   Of course: for a windy day.

TOM BROWN   And all of the windy nights too, right?

MAUDE SMITH   Oh, right. The windy nights are very important to think about. I have a strange funny feeling that tonight is going to be a windy night. Don't you think I'm right?

TOM BROWN *begins to make gunshot sounds with his voice as* HE *rocks furiously on his rocking horse: making believe to be shooting with one of his pistols.* MAUDE SMITH *begins to inspect the ranch house while* SHE *smokes her cigarette.*

TOM BROWN   You've never been wrong, Mother Maude.

MAUDE SMITH *is wandering around all over the place:* SHE *is like a dutiful mother making certain that her son's new home is in right order and keeping:* SHE *wants to correct anything that is wrong or uncomfortable or untidy.*

MAUDE SMITH   Of course, Tom Brown, maybe we shouldn't be here. Maybe we should go back to New York: Manhattan for you, and the Staten Island Ferry for me. I don't care what anyone else says . . .

TOM BROWN   Mother Maude: I love you! You knock me out!

MAUDE SMITH   I don't care what anyone else says: the Statue of Liberty still makes me cry whenever I see it!

TOM BROWN   I really love you! *(*TOM BROWN *rocks like half-a-mad-man now)*

MAUDE SMITH   Your place is very posh. It is very elegant. It's very impressive. It's very expensive. It looks like a picture out of a magazine.

TOM BROWN   *(Rocking)* Ya-hoo! *Ya-hoo! Yaaa-hooo!*

MAUDE SMITH *turns to face* TOM BROWN.

MAUDE SMITH   Tom Brown: you were always a crazy adorable little kid!

TOM BROWN   *(Rocking faster)* Ya-hoo! *Ya-hoo! Yaaa-hooo!*

MAUDE SMITH   But this place is posh in a gaudy way. It's elegant in a cheap way. It's impressive in a false way. It's expensive in an offensive way. And it looks like a picture out of a rotten magazine. *(Begins to dust off the empty rocking horses with her dainty silk handkerchief)*

TOM BROWN   *(Rocking even faster than before)* Ya-hoo! *Ya-hoo! Yaaa-hooo! (*HE *makes an incredible barrage of shooting sounds now)*

MAUDE SMITH   *(Dusting)* I'm trying to fix your place up a bit before your girl friend arrives.

TOM BROWN   Wait until you meet her! She's wonderful, Mother Maude!

MAUDE SMITH   I wish you would stop calling me Mother Maude, Tom Brown.

TOM BROWN   What do you want me to call you then?

MAUDE SMITH   Just plain Maude is fine. Just the way you always did before.

TOM BROWN   Okay: *Maude!* (TOM BROWN *is rocking very furiously again*) Guess what, Maude?!

MAUDE SMITH *continues to dust the rocking horses.*

MAUDE SMITH   Yes, Tom Brown?

TOM BROWN   I'm getting an erection, Maude!

MAUDE SMITH   Tom Brown! You're not supposed to tell your mother things like that!

TOM BROWN   But Maude: an erection is such a good thing to have! (TOM BROWN *stops rocking abruptly;* HE *lights a cigarette*)

MAUDE SMITH   Well, I do believe in sex education among parents and their children. I think it's a good and healthy thing.

TOM BROWN   Then you're not embarrassed after all?

MAUDE SMITH   No, I'm not embarrassed.

TOM BROWN *jumps off his rocking horse.*

TOM BROWN   Sex education among parents is a good and healthy thing: and so is getting an erection, Maude.

MAUDE SMITH   Tom Brown: let's put on some television. (MAUDE SMITH *begins to look for the television set*)

TOM BROWN *jumps on the rocking horse belonging to Horace White.* HE *begins to rock on it.*

TOM BROWN   An erection is a real thing. It deals with so many things. Sometimes you get one because of your heart: and because of the way your heart feels. Sometimes you get one because of your head and your brain and your mind.

MAUDE SMITH *is still looking for the television set.*

MAUDE SMITH   Where in the world do you keep your television set, Tom Brown?

TOM BROWN   *(Still rocking away)* Just press the center of the wall back there. *(HE points to the center of the cyclorama)*

MAUDE SMITH *goes to it and presses an invisible button. Immediately the whole cyclorama changes before your eyes: it is now a vast watercolor of a lush green forest: it should take our breaths away.*

MAUDE SMITH   Oh, what a lovely channel this is! Tom: look at it: isn't it just beautiful?!

TOM BROWN *jumps off the rocking horse;* HE *takes a long drag on his cigarette;* HE *glances at the cyclorama and smiles.*

Life can be so fucking divine!

TOM BROWN *jumps on the rocking horse belonging to Sheriff Sunshine:* HE *rocks like a happy lunatic.*

TOM BROWN   Life can always be divine period: if you just give a fuck period!

MAUDE SMITH *is enthralled with the lush green forest.* SHE *crushes her cigarette out on the floor with her foot, and then* SHE *lights up a new one.* SHE *begins to walk from our left to our right: following the cyclorama.*

MAUDE SMITH   I brought you up right, Tom Brown.

TOM BROWN   *(Rocking fast)* Sometimes you get an erection just by being brought up right. My God, Maude! Sometimes you can get an erection just by looking at trees period! It's as plain and simple as that, Maude. Do you know what I mean!

MAUDE SMITH   Do you know what I miss most of all, Tom Brown?
I miss when you were small and I used to go out and buy all of
your underwear: that's what I miss most of all. I personally think
that all mothers miss that most of all. You certainly wore out all
your underwear in such short periods of time. *(By now* MAUDE
SMITH *has carefully studied the whole vast cyclorama of the
gigantic expanse of rich green trees)*

TOM BROWN   *(Still rocking fast)* I mean: do you know what I mean,
Maude?

*The sweet semi-somber strumming of the lone guitar is now
dying away.* TOM BROWN *jumps off Sheriff Sunshine's rocking
horse.* HE *dashes to* MAUDE SMITH: HE *hugs her;* HE *kisses her.*

Maude . . . ? I'm in trouble. I'm not happy. I need you to help
me.

MAUDE SMITH   I'll always be here in order to help you, Tom Brown.
*(*MAUDE SMITH *gently breaks away from him)* I adore your television set! Do you mind if I switch to another channel?

TOM BROWN   No: by all means. I rented this place for you, Maude.
I had this special television set installed just for you. I want to
make sure you're pleased and happy as much as possible.

MAUDE SMITH   That's all very kind of you. *(*MAUDE SMITH *goes to
the center of the cyclorama)*

TOM BROWN   I'm in love, Maude. I'm in love with this very beautiful
girl.

MAUDE SMITH   Did I ever meet her?

MAUDE SMITH *presses the invisible television button at the center
of the cyclorama. This time the whole vast background turns into
a breathtaking picture of one of America's great rivers: most
likely: the Hudson River around West Point and/or the Bear*

Mountain Bridge: and we can tell that it is autumn at its most colorful and vivid height. MAUDE SMITH *swoons: and after a second or two* SHE *swoons again: only it is louder and longer . . . and then* TOM BROWN *swoons with her.* MAUDE SMITH *crushes her cigarette out on the floor, and then* TOM BROWN *does the same thing with his. Now* SHE *takes out another cigarette.* HE *lights it for her; then* HE *takes another one out for himself and* HE *lights it for himself. During all of this* THEY *are still swooning and broadly inspecting the whole of the lovely scene on the cyclorama. By this time the sweet semi-somber strumming of the lone guitar has died away completely. There is a marvelous peaceful silence: once* THEY *both stop their nicely-sounding swooning. And the lights on the cyclorama have begun to change into a delicious warm orange glare of the country during the fall.*

TOM BROWN   I'm in love with Abigail Pepper, Maude.

MAUDE SMITH   I know Abigail Pepper, Tom.

TOM BROWN   I know you do. Do you like her?

MAUDE SMITH   Oh, I love her. I mean: if you're in love with her, then I couldn't simply like her: I'd have to love her.

TOM BROWN   I'm glad to hear that, Maude. She's due here any minute now. She's coming to the party too. It's going to be a small party. It's for you and Abigail and me . . . and I've invited Horace White too. I've invited him for *you.*

MAUDE SMITH   Oh, my! I don't know what to do! I know Horace White too: he's a very sexy man. Do you know what he did the first time I met him? He buried me up in the sand. I met him at Jones Beach last summer. He's a very sexy man. I'm getting very nervous because I'm beginning to wonder how he feels about me. It seems as though it's much harder for a woman my age to be sexy than it is for a man the same age to be sexy.

THEY *are puffing away nervously now.*

TOM BROWN   Everything's going to turn out perfectly, Maude.

MAUDE SMITH   I hope you're right. Tom. *(MAUDE SMITH begins to fuss half-hysterically with her hairdo. She does it with the hand that holds the lit cigarette. She awkwardly singes a bit of her hair)* Oh, dear! Tom. . . ? !

TOM BROWN *presses with his hand at the section of singed hair.*

TOM BROWN   Please, Maude: that's very careless of you: and it's also very dangerous. *(TOM BROWN takes her cigarette from her hand and crushes it on the floor)*

MAUDE SMITH   I'm sorry, Tom. . . .

HE *gives her a son's kiss lightly on her lips.*

TOM BROWN   They should be arriving any minute now.

Suddenly: a large half-moon cut out of thick cardboard and painted a deep orange comes dropping slowly by a long string about the center of the stage where it finally stops and remains hanging in mid-air above their heads.

MAUDE SMITH   They're coming! I can hear them! How do I look?! *(MAUDE SMITH rapidly takes out another cigarette and lights it herself)*

TOM BROWN   You look perfectly fine, Maude.

And now a number of deep orange-colored stars, all of them various sizes but none as large as the half-moon, also come dropping down from long strings: finally resting and dangling in their scattered positions in mid-air above their hands and the rocking horses.

MAUDE SMITH   I'm so goddam fucking nervous, Tom!

TOM BROWN   I'm so goddam fucking nervous too, Maude!

This time we hear the lone guitar again: but it is loud and lingering: as though it is meant to make some sort of special theatrical announcement for some very particular occasion.

MAUDE SMITH   I wish I were back at Jones Beach: buried in the cozy sand!

The whole scene is very wealthy with the color of comfortable orange now.

TOM BROWN   *(Calling)* Come in! Come in!

MAUDE SMITH   *(Mumbling)* Oh, Tom . . . Tom . . . I hope I make a good impression . . . that's all . . .

TOM BROWN   You will, you will, Maude . . . and Christ, good Christ: I hope I make a good impression too . . . even half-a-good-impression! *(TOM BROWN straightens up like a big man or/and a big well-built soldier. Firmly)* I said to come in. Come in!!

MAUDE SMITH   *(Whispering to the stars and the moon)* Oh, dear God up in Heaven: please make them like me . . . please make them accept me . . . I'm not that bad, am I, God. . . ?

TOM BROWN   *(A louder whisper: looking straight ahead)* Please: dear God: make them like us.

The lone guitar reaches a fantastic peak of delightful strumming. HORACE WHITE *enters from our left.* HE *is smoking a cigarette.*

HORACE WHITE   Good evening, everybody!

MAUDE SMITH *gasps softly.* SHE *dashes to the center of the cyclorama.*

TOM BROWN   Hello, Horace White. How are you?

HORACE WHITE   I never felt better in my whole life! I've been looking forward to this little get-together!

MAUDE SMITH *presses another one of the invisible television buttons. This time the giant image changes into a lovely picture of the middle of the blue and white Atlantic Ocean at sunset.*

TOM BROWN   Maude. . . ?

MAUDE SMITH   Yes. . . ?

HORACE WHITE   Hello, Maude! You look better than ever!

MAUDE SMITH *begins to come forward again.*

MAUDE SMITH   I do. . . ?

HORACE WHITE   You certainly do!

MAUDE SMITH   Thank you . . .

TOM BROWN   We're expecting one other person. We're expecting Abigail Pepper. Do you know Abigail Pepper, Horace?

HORACE WHITE   I met her at the races once. She's a very good-looking girl, don't you think?

TOM BROWN   I think so.

MAUDE SMITH   She's lovely. And I'm so proud and happy that my son Tom Brown is in love with her. And I'll be even more proud and happy when they finally become man and wife.

TOM BROWN   If she'll have me, Maude.

MAUDE SMITH   She'll have you: don't be so negative, Tom.

HORACE WHITE   You have a fantastic place here, Tom.

TOM BROWN Thank you.

MAUDE SMITH It's nice and refreshing, don't you think?

HORACE WHITE Very nice and very refreshing. But I personally think that everything and everywhere and everybody and so on can be very nice and very refreshing if you really want to believe that: I mean if you really want to go along with that sort of attitude: which, by the way: is the only attitude I know of that makes pefect sense. I've come here to your son Tom Brown's party because I wanted to see you again, Maude Smith. I met you once in the sand at Jones Beach: and you've been on my mind ever since. Yes, Maude Smith: I came here tonight from the Northeast because I had a very certain attitude that I've been living with and feeding off of ever since that afternoon at Jones Beach in the afternoon sunshine of the crazy wild East Coast. I don't want to boast or anything like that, Maude Smith: but I knew how much I won you over: and that meant so much to me. Of course you don't know the other side of the story: you won me over in an even deeper way than I won you. You've been on my brain for one helluva long fucking time. My first wife was killed in a seven-car collision on the Florida highways well over five years ago now . . . and well: it's about time I fell in love again. (HE *pauses*) I'm sorry. I'm apologizing if I'm embarrassing either one of you.

MAUDE SMITH *looks as though* SHE *might burst into tears because* SHE *is so overcome with flattery and happiness.*

TOM BROWN Why don't you have a seat, Horace White?

HORACE WHITE Thank you. Don't mind if I do. (HORACE WHITE *sits down on his rocking horse and then* HE *begins to rock, puffing away on his cigarette.* HE *looks over at some of the watercolor picture on the cyclorama)*

That's a beautiful program you got on that channel, Maude, really beautiful.

MAUDE SMITH *crushes out her cigarette on the floor with her foot.*
HORACE WHITE *rocks faster now: full-straddle and really roaring to go.* TOM BROWN *crushes his cigarette out on the floor too.*

But then again: it's a beautiful life: what more can I tell you? In fact: it's so beautiful that I've been taking up the supreme and pure art of writing poetry these last few months. I've been writing poems about the moon and the sun and the stars and the forests and the oceans and the animals, and, of course, the *human beings* of the whole world too! Poetry is good for a man when he gets to be my age. I'm beginning to think that maybe poems should be written by the old folks rather than the young folks. Yes, the young folks should spend more of their time making human contacts while the older folks should spend more of their time enjoying the wonderful pleasures of recording all their human contacts of the past in the form of poems on any available paper within their reach. *(*HE *rocks very fast now)* It's a poetic life, let me tell you! And that's all there is to it!

MAUDE SMITH *lights up a new cigarette, and so does* TOM BROWN.

TOM BROWN   I'm certainly glad that I invited you to my party.

MAUDE SMITH   *(Hardly audible)* It's a poetic life . . .

HORACE WHITE *is somewhere else now: as* HE *rocks/rides away on his rocking horse.*

TOM BROWN   *(To himself)* It's going to be a poetic party full of poetic people thinking poetic poems because of these poetic times we all live in these days full of poems.

MAUDE SMITH   Oh, Tom Brown . . .

TOM BROWN   Yes, Maude Smith. . . ?

MAUDE SMITH   I think . . . I think . . . I'm going to faint! *(And then, that's what* MAUDE SMITH *does:* SHE *faints, falling easily onto the floor)*

TOM BROWN   Mama! Mother! Mother Maude! *(*TOM BROWN *runs to where* SHE *has passed out.* HORACE *is still somewhere else on his rocking horse)* Mama: it's Tommie!

The setting begins to change colors now: it is turning into an incredibly beautiful early-night light royal blue. The orange half-moon and the orange stars are slowly pulled up by their strings until we no longer see them. The lone guitar begins to play something resembling a nocturnal blues type of melody: it is sweet and nostalgic and perhaps a bit just right in being sentimental also. TOM BROWN *is trying to revive* MAUDE SMITH.

Maude, Maude, Maude. . . ? !

HORACE WHITE   *(Rocking like a crazy cowboy) Ya-hoo! Ya-hoo! Ya-hoo!*

TOM BROWN   Mama: why don't you come to?

HORACE WHITE *pretends* HE *is about to rope a head of cattle.*

HORACE WHITE   *(Screaming happily)* I'm not going to harm you, cow! I'm your friend really! Just playing a stupid role, that's all! I love you: cow!

And now a new moon comes down into our view. It is also dangling from a long string. But this moon is a full moon; it is also a shimmering grey rather than the rich orange before it.

TOM BROWN   Maude?! Abigail's arrived! I'm a little scared, Mama!

We now notice a bunch of new variously-sized scattered stars coming down into our view above the three heads of the people at the party, dangling from long strings as well, but this time the stars are also shimmering grey rather than the rich orange of before: it is a precious-looking cardboard galaxy of make-believe. To our left we notice ABIGAIL PEPPER. SHE *has just arrived: and* SHE *is smoking.*

ABIGAIL PEPPER   Here I am. I'm sorry I'm late. Oh, what a lovely looking place! Where did you get that television set? It's simply incredible. And the picture is simply remarkable: let alone the lovely fact that its subject matter at the moment is so lovely-looking, to say the least! *(*SHE *begins to walk about the place)* And your furniture?! It's so terribly interesting, to say the loveli-est least: so terribly intriguing, your lovely-looking furniture, and the way it's all so perfectly preciously arranged. I'm completely overwhelmed already: and the party hasn't really even begun as yet. I don't know whether I can take all of this beauty in one night. I'm absolutely astounded, and, to say the most beautiful least: I'm simply enchanted like I have never ever been en-chanted before in my whole short young life so far!

HORACE WHITE *is beginning to slow down his rocking/riding;* HE *is vaguely aware that* ABIGAIL PEPPER *has arrived.* TOM BROWN *gets up from his kneeling position and then* HE *nervously goes to* ABIGAIL PEPPER. HE *takes her hands in his, and then* HE *kisses her lightly on the lips.*

TOM BROWN   My mother's passed out, Abigail.

ABIGAIL PEPPER   That's terrible, Tom.

ABIGAIL PEPPER *breaks away from* TOM BROWN*'s handholding and goes to* MAUDE SMITH. SHE *bends over her.* SHE *lifts* MAUDE*'s head up.* SHE *takes her own lit cigarette and begins to force it into* MAUDE*'s closed mouth.* TOM BROWN *now approaches the two of them.*

TOM BROWN   What are you doing, Abigail Pepper?

ABIGAIL PEPPER   This will help her, Tom.

ABIGAIL PEPPER *has managed to get the lit cigarette into* MAUDE SMITH *'s mouth so that now* MAUDE *can begin to puff on it: which* SHE *does.*

There, you see?! She's coming to! Everything will be all right, Tom, I promise you.

TOM BROWN   I wouldn't know what to do without you, Abigail Pepper.

By now the blues-type melody of the lone guitar player has ended.

ABIGAIL PEPPER   How are you, Maude? Are you feeling all right now, Maude?

MAUDE *begins to puff away on the lit cigarette that* ABIGAIL *forced into her mouth.* SHE *tries to lift her head up;* ABIGAIL *helps her lift it up.*

TOM BROWN   You okay, Maude?

TOM BROWN *goes to where* MAUDE SMITH *is now sitting up and where* ABIGAIL PEPPER *is kneeling down beside her.* ABIGAIL *now borrows the cigarette from* MAUDE *taking a few long drags on it.* HORACE *has stopped rocking completely now:* HE *jumps off the rocking horse.*

HORACE WHITE   You okay, Maude? *(*HORACE WHITE *goes to* MAUDE SMITH *and helps her get to her feet)*

MAUDE SMITH   You're a real gentleman.

HORACE WHITE   I'm going to write a long epic-type poem about you someday, Maude: a real winner-of-a-poem!

MAUDE SMITH   You're a real winner-of-a-gentleman, Horace White.

TOM BROWN *leads* ABIGAIL PEPPER *away from them.*

ABIGAIL PEPPER   It's such a delicious, such a luscious-looking-feeling home that you have here, Tom.

TOM BROWN   That's what you are, Abigail Pepper: such a luscious-looking-feeling woman! Such a *delicious* luscious-looking-feeling woman!

ABIGAIL PEPPER   But I must tell you something, Tom. I must tell you something that might bother you a whole lot. It might disturb you a whole lot, in fact.

ABIGAIL PEPPER *takes out a new cigarette.* TOM BROWN *lights it for her.*

Thank you, Tom. . . .

TOM BROWN   Nothing you could tell me could ever disturb me . . . nothing!

HORACE WHITE *takes* MAUDE SMITH *by the hand.* HE *leads her to his rocking horse.*

HORACE WHITE   Let's go for a ride together, okay, Maude?

MAUDE SMITH   I'd love to do it!

HORACE WHITE *jumps onto the rocking horse first: full-straddle.* HE *lights up a new cigarette as* HE *does so.*

HORACE WHITE   All right, honey: now it's your turn to get on with me.

TOM BROWN *lights up a new cigarette for himself.*

ABIGAIL PEPPER   Tom. . . ?

MAUDE SMITH Here I come, honey! *(*MAUDE SMITH *manages to jump upon the rocking horse: side-saddle in front of* HORACE WHITE*)*

TOM BROWN What's the matter, Abby?

HORACE WHITE Yippeee!

MAUDE SMITH Yippeee!

ABIGAIL PEPPER I've got a bad heart!

HORACE WHITE *Yippeee!*

MAUDE SMITH *Yippeee!*

TOM BROWN What did you say?

ABIGAIL PEPPER *I've got a bad heart!*

TOM BROWN What do you mean, Abby?

ABIGAIL PEPPER My heart is in terrible shape at the moment. The doctors tell me I can die at a very young age if I'm not careful, if I don't take care of myself.

TOM BROWN That's awful!

ABIGAIL PEPPER I may not even be able to have any children . . . ever!

TOM BROWN That's *really* awful!

HORACE WHITE *and* MAUDE SMITH *are both rocking together now.*

MAUDE SMITH What are you going to call the long epic poem that you're going to write for me? I mean: do you have any idea for a title yet?

HORACE WHITE   I think it will be a long title!

MAUDE SMITH   Oh?

HORACE WHITE   A very long title! In fact: the title itself will tell a story in itself. It will whet people's appetites. I mean: do you know what I mean, Maude?

TOM BROWN   Why don't you sit down, Abby? Please, have a seat, okay?

MAUDE SMITH   I don't quite know what you mean.

ABIGAIL PEPPER   I'd love to have a seat.

TOM BROWN *leads* ABIGAIL PEPPER *to his rocking horse.*

HORACE WHITE   I mean that nowadays, in these cold times that we all live in, well, in order to write an epic poem these days, or even a little simple poem for that matter: well, we got to whet people's appetites first, just because we have to somehow force them to even read a new poem these days. . . .

MAUDE SMITH   Or even old poems!

HORACE WHITE   You're absolutely right, Maude!

TOM BROWN *jumps onto his rocking horse: full-straddle.*

TOM BROWN   Let me help you get on, Abby. *(*TOM BROWN *extends his hands and then* HE *helps* ABIGAIL PEPPER *climb onto his rocking horse side-saddle)*

ABIGAIL PEPPER   This is going to be fun! I can tell how much fun it's going to be!

TOM BROWN *and* ABIGAIL PEPPER *begin to rock/ride alongside of the rocking/riding* HORACE WHITE *and* MAUDE SMITH.

TOM BROWN   Yippeee!

ABIGAIL PEPPER   Yippeee!

TOM BROWN *and* ABIGAIL PEPPER *begin to giggle together:* THEY *are both having a good solid time of it.*

MAUDE SMITH   Just look at them, will you, Horace? Just look at the children! Aren't they lovely to look at? Aren't they lovely and luscious and lilting and loving to see?!

HORACE WHITE   They make a lovely luscious lilting loving pair, don't they?

TOM BROWN   *Yippeee!*

ABIGAIL PEPPER   *Yippeee!*

HORACE WHITE   *Yippeee!*

MAUDE SMITH   *Yippeee!*

TOM BROWN   Abigail?!

ABIGAIL PEPPER   Yes?

TOM BROWN   I love your heart!

MAUDE SMITH   Listen to him! Listen to my beautiful son! Such a perfect gentleman!

HORACE WHITE   *Yippeee!*

TOM BROWN   I love your good bad heart! And I love your soul, and your eyes and nose and mouth and lips and teeth and neck and

and hair and arms and breasts and belly and belly button and *cunt!*

HORACE WHITE   I don't know about that. . . .

TOM BROWN   Your extra-good cunt . . .

MAUDE SMITH   He's speaking the way a man should speak. He's speaking out in the open. He's saying the things that a woman needs to hear. He's honest!

>   TOM BROWN *and* ABIGAIL PEPPER *now indulge in a long extended sort-of-innocently-passionate embrace as* THEY *rock easily on the rocking horse.* MAUDE SMITH *manages to get off the rocking horse and away from* HORACE WHITE.

HORACE WHITE   What's the trouble, Maude?

>   MAUDE SMITH *walks to the center of the cyclorama where the invisible television button is.*

MAUDE SMITH   I want to find a new channel, that's all. There's nothing wrong, really.

>   HORACE WHITE *jumps off his rocking horse.*

HORACE WHITE   There is too: I can certainly tell that there is something wrong. You're troubled, Maude Smith. Maybe I can help you.

>   HORACE WHITE *begins to head toward where* MAUDE SMITH *is standing.* TOM BROWN *and* ABIGAIL PEPPER *continue in their "mad" embrace on their rocking rocking horse.*

MAUDE SMITH   You're a good man, Horace: I can tell. I believe that you're a very good man.

HORACE WHITE   And I can tell that you're a good woman, Maude: a very good woman.

HORACE WHITE *crushes his cigarette out on the floor with his foot.* HE *reaches* MAUDE SMITH. HE *takes her cigarette and also crushes it out on the floor with his foot.*

MAUDE SMITH Such an extremely good man you are!

MAUDE SMITH *gives him a light peck on the forehead, and then* HORACE WHITE *gives her a light peck on each one of her cheeks.* THEY *both smile now: it is a very warm and friendly and lovingly respectful smile on both their parts.*

HORACE WHITE Such an extremely good woman you are!

HORACE WHITE *takes hold of* MAUDE SMITH*'s hand. And then, with her other hand,* MAUDE *presses the imaginary television button in the center of the cyclorama. The picture changes. This time we see a glistening scene of fresh-fallen snow covering the beautiful countryside: lots of large and tiny evergreen trees and other trees as well, and numerous-type bushes, and perhaps a farmhouse in the distance, along with the clean clear sky of very early morning with the sunshine breaking through the thin and skimpy clouds.* MAUDE SMITH *swoons, and then* HORACE WHITE *swoons with her.* THEY *both hold hands: swooning together, as* THEY *inspect the wholeness of the lovely image on the sprawling cyclorama. And every so often, on their little trip, the two of them continue to exchange childish kisses back and forth. And* TOM BROWN *and* ABIGAIL PEPPER *continue in their "mad" embrace on the tenderly rocking rocking horse.*

MAUDE SMITH My son, Tom Brown. . . ?

HORACE WHITE Yes. . . ?

MAUDE SMITH He has a bad heart. . . .

HORACE WHITE A bad heart. . . ?

MAUDE SMITH I mean: it's a good heart because he's a son and a good man and a good person. . . .

HORACE WHITE   Yes. . . ?

MAUDE SMITH   But his heart is *bad* physically, physically, physically.

HORACE WHITE   It's hard to believe, Maude. It's hard to accept. It's all very hard because he's just a young man.

MAUDE SMITH   But that's the way it is: it's the truth, the reality: the awful fact is that my good son with his good heart has a bad heart: physically. I don't know what to do, Horace White. I just simply don't know what to do.

>   MAUDE SMITH *begins to sob a little bit.* HORACE WHITE *makes an attempt at consoling her.*

HORACE WHITE   But that's all right, Maude. It's okay. It's only physical. That's nothing: physical. It means nothing: physical. It's a good solid heart despite everything else. *Good and solid!* The physical part means nothing; the physical part might even be evil, and so we should forget it if it's evil, because it doesn't count. Do you know what I'm saying to you, Maude?

>   *There is a short pause.*

MAUDE SMITH   Yes. I think I know what you mean, Horace.

>   HORACE *leads* MAUDE *back to his rocking horse.*

HORACE WHITE   Where shall we go?

MAUDE SMITH   Wherever you want to go.

>   HORACE WHITE *jumps back onto his rocking horse. Then* HE *takes* MAUDE SMITH *by the hand and helps her to climb back on as well: sitting in front of him, side-saddle.*

HORACE WHITE   Yippeee!

MAUDE SMITH Yippeee!

MAUDE SMITH *wipes her tears. At the moment* THEY *are not yet rocking/riding the rocking horse.* HORACE WHITE *takes out two cigarettes.* HE *lights one for* MAUDE *and then* HE *lights one for himself. And now* THEY *begin to rock/ride the rocking horse.*

HORACE WHITE It will be a good trip!

MAUDE SMITH I need a good trip! Of course I need a good trip with someone like you!

HORACE WHITE That's very nice of you!

MAUDE SMITH Thank you!

There is a silent pause as THEY *continue to rock/ride and while* TOM BROWN *and* ABIGAIL PEPPER *continue their "mad" embrace on their own separate rocking horse: which is almost at a complete standstill now. And if it can be honestly and pleasantly said—without embarrassment, and with nice acceptance instead—the whole of the cyclorama is beginning to resemble a vague image of a Norman Rockwell painting perhaps. And the lights are growing more into the bright hues of a clear crisp winter night in America. And now:* HORACE WHITE *and* MAUDE SMITH *really begin their trip by starting to rock/ride on their active little rocking horse. The pause continues on until finally* HORACE WHITE *decides to break into it.*

HORACE WHITE Maude Smith. . . ?

MAUDE SMITH Yes, Horace White. . . ? *(Another short pause)* I said: 'Yes, Horace White?' *(Another short pause)*

HORACE WHITE I love you. I'm in love with you: very much! I love you because I've fallen in love with you! And do you know what that means?

MAUDE SMITH *is beaming like a schoolgirl.*

It means that I am going to have to pop the question. *Pop!*
Maude: will you . . . marry me? Will you be my wife, Maude?

MAUDE SMITH *nearly falls off the rocking horse, but* HORACE
WHITE *makes certain that* SHE *doesn't.*

MAUDE SMITH   *(Wholly ecstatic)* Yippeee!

HORACE WHITE *begins to laugh.* THEY *both puff extravagantly on
their cigarettes.*

HORACE WHITE   Yippeee!

Now THEY *both nearly fall off the rocking horse together. But*
THEY *manage not to after all. It is a lovely romantic incredibly
wonderful childlike struggle.* TOM BROWN *and* ABIGAIL PEPPER
finally come out of their "mad" embrace. THEY *both stare at each
other for a long time and as they do* THEY *begin to rock/ride their
rocking horse together.*

TOM BROWN   It would be so nice, Abigail Pepper, to see you without
your clothes on. Do you know what I mean? I would love to help
you undress and I would love for you to help me undress too.
It would be so nice, don't you think, Abby?

At this moment, HORACE WHITE *and* MAUDE SMITH *go into a sort
of "mad" embrace, similar to the one that we just watched* TOM
BROWN *and* ABIGAIL PEPPER *pull out of.*

ABIGAIL PEPPER   I should be ashamed, but I'm not.

TOM BROWN   Well, I'd be very disappointed if you were ashamed,
Abby.

ABIGAIL PEPPER   It would be so nice, wouldn't it? The two of us
entirely naked from head to foot: studying one another's beauti-

ful naked bodies in the light of the moon or the sun, in a
bedroom or on a beach, or in a bathroom, or sitting together
while we have breakfast in a warm cozy kitchen.

TOM BROWN   We can do it, you know?!

ABIGAIL PEPPER   We can. . . ?!

TOM BROWN   Of course we can! You see: I'm in love with you,
Abby!

ABIGAIL PEPPER   I feel exactly the same way about you, Tom.

TOM BROWN   It's marvelous, isn't it?

ABIGAIL PEPPER   Do you want to know something? My heart feels
perfectly fine at the moment. I mean it never felt so marvelous
before.

TOM BROWN   Where shall we go?

ABIGAIL PEPPER   Anywhere *you* want to go!

TOM BROWN   Make a suggestion.

ABIGAIL PEPPER   Well, we could ride . . . naked of course. . . .

TOM BROWN   Naked, of course!

ABIGAIL PEPPER   Well, we could ride to our gigantic house on top
of our gigantic hill that overlooks the gorgeous green rims of our
radiant red canyon that is so perfectly surrounded by our own
private and very special forest of yellow trees covered everywhere
with all sorts of new colored leaves and the strangest and weird-
est and most beautiful flowers in the whole world. How about
that, Tom Brown? Doesn't that excite you?! I mean just the
mere thought of it all?!

TOM BROWN   It also is making me come: the mere thought of it all!

ABIGAIL PEPPER   I'm ashamed to admit it: but me too!

THEY *both laugh together as* THEY *both really begin to rock/ride together now.*

TOM BROWN   I want you, that's all! I don't want anybody else! I never wanted anybody else in my entire life!

TOM BROWN *takes out a cigarette each for the two of them;* HE *lights them both and then* THEY *begin to puff away.*

ABIGAIL PEPPER   Screw my bad heart, that's what I say!

TOM BROWN   And just in case I've got a bad heart too, like you, then I say: screw it too! In fact: I say: fuck it! Fuck my bad heart, because at heart: well, it's really a very good heart at heart!

ABIGAIL PEPPER   Oh, God: I know it is!

TOM BROWN *takes* ABIGAIL PEPPER *in his arms and* THEY *go back into another "mad" embrace matching the one that* HORACE WHITE *and* MAUDE SMITH *are still indulging in. A few moments go by. And then the huge sprawling winter night scene on the vast cyclorama suddenly begins to flutter and blink; and then it begins to fade; and then finally it is out completely. The setting is somewhat dark and rather dismal-looking now.* HORACE WHITE *breaks away from* MAUDE SMITH *and all of a sudden* THEY *are both coughing together. And then* TOM BROWN *and* ABIGAIL PEPPER *break out of their "mad" embrace also; and* THEY *also both begin to cough together. The coughing of the four of them all at the same time is very disturbing: it is disturbing for them and it is disturbing for us.* THEY *all cough and cough and cough. And then one by one, as though in slow motion:* THEY *all fall off the two rocking horses and onto the floor, where* THEY *are coughing even more than before: rolling about on the stage: coughing louder and louder and almost violently; and by now* THEY *have*

*all rid themselves of their smoking cigarettes. Each one of them
manages to crush his cigarettes out on the floor, with his hands
this time. The coughing gets louder now and is also now out of
any sort of resemblance to control.* SHERIFF SUNSHINE *enters to
our left.* HE *is smoking a cigarette.*

SHERIFF SUNSHINE   What's going on here? This is terrible! I was told
to report here. An awful lot of complaints from the neighbors
everywhere. This is terrible! I came over here on my motorcycle
because all of the reports said: "disturbing the peace." This is
really quite terrible! It's also sad! And what it all really boils
down to is this: it's a tragedy! A real tragedy! Now the point is
this: the four of you must control yourselves. The four of you
must stop disturbing the peace of the neighborhood, and all of
the surrounding areas as well. My God: this is a terrible tragedy!
What the hell can I do to help you people? Good Christ: I hate
my job. I hate being a sheriff. I hate being Sheriff Sunshine. This
job, in cases such as this, has absolutely nothing to do with the
warm sunshine. I'll tell you all something: I wish I had someone
to love. I wish I was in love with someone, and I wish someone
was also in love with me. Listen: do you people have a television
set around here? We've got to find some form of concentration
so that the four of you will stop all of this terrible tragic coughing. Now if I had a young girl to make love to everytime I wanted
to make love, and everytime she wanted to make love, which,
of course, would always have to be the right time, the right time
being when we both wanted to make love because we both were
in love with each other . . . *well:* if this were the case now, then
things would be different, wouldn't they now? This is a terrible
tragic case. My God! People wouldn't believe this if they even
saw it with their own eyes, would they now?

HORACE WHITE, MAUDE SMITH, TOM BROWN, *and* ABIGAIL PEP-
PER *are still coughing: violently now: all in set sitting positions
amid the quiet and still rocking horses.* SHERIFF SUNSHINE *begins
to look for a television set.* HE *does so by feeling the surface of
the vast cyclorama.* HE *feels and feels and feels. And now* HE *is
near the center of it: where the invisible television button exists.*

HE *feels there too. And just as soon as* HE *does: a fantastic picture comes suddenly on. It is the most beautiful and the most breath-taking scene of them all. It is a vast and lingering field or meadow on a bright summer's day and it is so rich and lush with all of the flowers in the world imaginable. It is almost hard to believe! And as the scene appears before our dazzled eyes we hear the sounds of a little shower of rain coming from somewhere.* SHER-IFF SUNSHINE *is most impressed: to say the very least.* HE *is very proud that he has found this particular channel.* HE *begins to inspect the whole cyclorama, as if* HE *is studying and enjoying the world's best and most celebrated painting. By now:* HORACE WHITE *has managed to get to his feet, and* HE *has assisted* MAUDE SMITH *in getting up on her two feet as well.* THEY *have both stopped coughing now, and* THEY *both stand side by side, and it makes us think of the statue-type couples atop a tall wedding cake. And by now:* TOM BROWN *and* ABIGAIL PEPPER *have gone through the same "ritual" as well, and* THEY *also resemble the statue-type couples atop a tall wedding cake.* SHERIFF SUNSHINE *moves down and stands between the two couples.* HE *takes his burning cigarette and tosses it to the floor.* HE *then crushes it with his foot.*

MAUDE SMITH   What a lovely day in such a lovely life!

HORACE WHITE   It certainly is lovely, isn't it?!

ABIGAIL PEPPER   I'm really incredibly happy!

TOM BROWN   So am I!

SHERIFF SUNSHINE *goes to* HORACE WHITE *and* MAUDE SMITH. HE *takes* HORACE*'s hand in his.*

SHERIFF SUNSHINE   Do you, Horace White, take Maude Smith as your lovable and loving wife?

HORACE WHITE   I do. . . .

SHERIFF SUNSHINE *now takes* MAUDE SMITH*'s hand in his.*

SHERIFF SUNSHINE   Do you, Maude Smith, take Horace White as
your lovable and loving husband?

MAUDE SMITH   I do. . . .

SHERIFF SUNSHINE *moves away from them and goes to*
TOM BROWN *and* ABIGAIL PEPPER. HE *takes* TOM*'s hand in
his.*

SHERIFF SUNSHINE   Do you, Tom Brown, take Abigail Pepper as
your lovable and loving wife?

TOM BROWN   I do. . . .

SHERIFF SUNSHINE *takes* ABIGAIL*'s hand in his.*

SHERIFF SUNSHINE   Do you, Abigail Pepper, take Tom Brown as
your lovable and loving husband?

ABIGAIL PEPPER   I do. . . .

SHERIFF SUNSHINE *lets go of* ABIGAIL*'s hand. We notice that the
sound of the light shower of rain stops abruptly now.* SHERIFF
SUNSHINE *takes out a pair of extra-large dice.* HE *shakes them
firmly and steadily, like an old perfect pro, in his right hand.* HE
kisses his hand quickly as it still moves, and then HE *tosses the
dice onto the floor before him. The dice stop rolling and then*
SHERIFF SUNSHINE *looks down at them.* HE *smiles triumphantly.*
HE *bends over and picks up the dice. The lone guitar music,
sweeter than ever before, is heard in the background.* SHERIFF
SUNSHINE *turns to face* HORACE WHITE *and* MAUDE SMITH. HE
smiles so wonderfully at them.

SHERIFF SUNSHINE   Horace White and Maude Smith: I now pronounce you both man and wife.

HORACE WHITE *kisses* MAUDE SMITH *gently, and then* THEY *begin to dance together about the stage.*

Forever . . . ! *(*SHERIFF SUNSHINE *now turns to face* TOM BROWN *and* ABIGAIL PEPPER. HE *smiles so wonderfully at them too)* Tom Brown and Abigail Pepper: I now pronounce you both man and wife. Forever!

TOM BROWN *kisses* ABIGAIL PEPPER *gently, and then* THEY *begin to dance together about the stage as well. The lone guitar music does not sound so alone anymore. It is beginning to sound jazzier, rocky as rocky can be, and it certainly is not a lone guitar anymore. It is very now and very celebrating and very perfectly loud.*

SHERIFF SUNSHINE *takes his dice again.* HE *shakes them in his right hand.* HE *kisses his right hand right before tossing the dice onto the floor before him.* HE *looks to see what* HE *has thrown.* HE *smiles triumphantly.*

The full moon dangling from its long string is no longer greyish: it is very bright white . . . and so are the stars. And then the vast cyclorama begins to flicker, but the flickering is somewhat lovely and precious to see. The flickering consists of all the former scenes of all the former channels flickering beautifully before our eyes: over and over again. SHERIFF SUNSHINE *takes up the dice and shakes them in his right hand again. The flickering is very clear and very constant.*

HORACE WHITE *and* MAUDE SMITH *exchange partners with* TOM BROWN *and* ABIGAIL PEPPER. SHERIFF SUNSHINE *tosses the dice to the floor after instantly kissing his right hand.* HE *sees what he has made on the floor.* HE *is very pleased.* HORACE WHITE *and* MAUDE SMITH *resume their own partnership again, and so do* TOM BROWN *and* ABIGAIL PEPPER. SHERIFF SUNSHINE *picks up the dice again.* HORACE WHITE *and* MAUDE SMITH *begin to dance off to our left; and* TOM BROWN *and* ABIGAIL PEPPER *begin to dance off to our right.* SHERIFF SUNSHINE *begins shaking the dice in his right hand once more.* HORACE WHITE *and* MAUDE SMITH *are gone; and now* TOM BROWN *and* ABIGAIL PEPPER *are gone too.*

The loud lovely jazzy-rocky music stops: and immediately: the "Moonlight Serenade" theme plays as in the beginning of the play. And then, along with it, The Nitty Gritty Dirt Band with their version of "Hard-Hearted Hannah" is also heard playing: as though two jukeboxes are on at the same time. The former orange half-moon and all of the variously-shaped orange stars of before are lowered before our eyes again from their long dangling strings: joining the bright white full moon and the bright white stars: all dangling and jumping together above the whole setting. The flickering of the scenes on the cyclorama never stops.

SHERIFF SUNSHINE *is still shaking the dice;* HE *is shaking them like a crazy desperate man now. It seems like such a long frantic time. Finally:* HE *kisses his right hand, very firmly this time . . . and then* HE *lets the dice go rolling out onto the floor before him.*

And the curtain comes down terribly fast.

DIALECT DETERMINISM
Or: The Rally
Ed Bullins

Demagoguery, devilry, and death are the guts of *Dialect Determinism*, a toughly quiet piece of expressionist satire. Ed Bullins' love and concern for the memory of Malcolm X and the spirit of the black community give his acerbic picture of the traditional Harlem meeting hall a two-edged thrust: against the white oppression that creates division among blacks, and simultaneously against the black leaders who exploit divisiveness for their own ends and lull their people into false self-satisfaction.

and from below the podium BOSS BROTHER *withdraws a silver pitcher and pours a glass of pink lemonade into a tall glass, takes a drink and swishes the beverage about in his mouth before* HE *pulls back his head and swallows.*

A loud knocking sounds. Only the DOORMAN *notices.* HE *peers through the entrance as if he were looking through a peephole. (The door is imaginary.)*

VISITOR   *(From outside)* Good evening!

DOORMAN *makes motion of opening door a crack and allows the* VISITOR *to slip inside. A slamming noise is heard as the* DOORMAN *shuts the imaginary door.* BOSS BROTHER *jumps slightly at the sound and begins his speech.*

BOSS BROTHER   *(Mumbles)* We have come here, Brothers and Sisters, for a great purpose . . . haaaruump . . . ahh . . . yeah. . . . Let us commune.

BOSS BROTHER, BROTHERS *and* SISTERS *bow their heads and moan and groan.*

DOORMAN   *(To* VISITOR*)* Evening, Brother!

HE *shoves the* VISITOR *against a wall, having him stretch forward so that* HE *can frisk him.*

BOSS BROTHER   Let us commune in our hour of want, Brothers and Sisters.

DOORMAN   First time here?

The VISITOR *nods, bumping his forehead against the backdrop.*

If you'll just let me . . . *(*HE *frisks the* VISITOR *expertly)* Will you please empty your pockets out on that table?

As the curtain rises, Negro gospel music plays in a
A spotlight remains on BOSS BROTHER throughou
production, even when HE is not in the central ac
it diminishes in intensity and alters colors to
changes.

BOSS BROTHER stands upon a raised platform or a soa
left stage apron, midway between rows of folding
stage and the theater audience. The first row in the
part of the stage set, and BOSS BROTHER will sp
directions; HE wears a black woolly wig and a dark,
business suit. HE arranges papers upon the podiu
blackboard.

The BROTHERS and SISTERS file in from stage right and
the MEN on one side, the WOMEN on the other. W
seats are taken except for the one the VISITOR will
remaining BROTHERS and SISTERS file off the stage and
front row. The MEN wear green business suits, purple
orange ties; the WOMEN wear chic shifts of exotic patte
cal birds rustle amid purple foliage, across black shoul
grape leaves mottling azure and scarlet backgrounds.

The backdrop is an enormous likeness of The Serene
fact, it is a huge, stylized representation of an African m
word Peace is painted and displayed over the entire sta
word is stenciled upon the back of each chair, and som
MEN have the word sewed to the seats of their trousers

The DOORMAN does not take a seat but walks to the edge
stage and begins patrolling the length of the stage in a sem
step, much in the manner of an automaton. HE marches b
the entrance as BOSS BROTHER clears his throat and ratt
papers. From beneath a table which stands outside the ent
the DOORMAN takes a large picture of The Serene Man an
it upon the table.

The BROTHERS and SISTERS moan and hum to the weird m

The VISITOR *takes out wallet, cards, currency and miscellaneous items from pockets.* DOORMAN *places items in manila envelope.*

Now, I'll have to take these things. You'll get these back right after the meeting.

VISITOR   How?

DOORMAN   Because you are number one, Brother. *(Points)* Inside, please.

The BROTHERS' *and* SISTERS' *eyes fasten upon the* VISITOR *as* HE *walks to his seat, but* THEY *immediately return to meditation as* BOSS BROTHER *clears his throat.*

BOSS BROTHER   *(Croons and puts aside his papers)* I call you Brothers for we have a common experience and we shall share a common future, for we have common aspirations and common destinies. . . . As I've mentioned, so if our fates are shared, then we form a brotherhood, or for those of you who shun the unpleasantness you may find in this word, brotherhood, we will only say that we are here for mutual benefits . . . Brothers . . . ha ha ha. *(*BOSS BROTHER*'s movements are slow and flashy.* HE *uses a large white handkerchief to dab his puffy lips and to mop his forehead;* HE *waves the handkerchief like a banner whenever the* CROWD *becomes excited)* You see, it doesn't hurt to be identified with your own, I mean . . . it's not half as bad as some of you newer ones might suspect. *(His eyes seek out the* VISITOR*)*

LOUD BROTHER   *(Shouting to* BOSS BROTHER*) Tell us about it, Brother, talk about it!*

VOICES   Yeah, bring it on down front, man.

BOSS BROTHER   Yaasss . . . I see what you means, children.

LOUD BROTHER   *Give us the word, Brother!*

VOICES   Yes, the word!

A spot focuses upon the picture of The Serene Man and BOSS
BROTHER'*s spot vacillates as the tempo alters.*

BOSS BROTHER   *(Smiling)* Well, you know that nationalism ain't an
invention of bro. . . . Oh, sorry, I means of the black man
. . . Yawhl.

FIRST BROTHER   What yawhl say?

SECOND BROTHER   Let Brother speak!

BOSS BROTHER   It was with the rise of the European nation-states
that nationalism becomes evident in history. . . .

LOUD BROTHER   That's right!

YOUNG SISTER   It is! Can't you hear those big words he's using? He's
got to be right.

FIRST BROTHER   Right!

LOUD BROTHER   *That's right!*

SECOND BROTHER   Right!

VOICES   *Sho nuf!*

BOSS BROTHER *flutters his handkerchief and drinks his lemonade.
The* CROWD *sways with the wonder of the* SPEAKER; *it is an inner
rhythm rushing up to their heads from their stirring seats, to
smash out in explosive enthusiasm. Sitting still, the* VISITOR *pulls
his eyes away from the* SPEAKER'*s and focuses upon his feet.*

BOSS BROTHER   Now in unity we have found by looking at history
there is strength . . . in brotherhood there is power, and all we
want is power, don't we's, just like everybody else? . . . So as de

most honest people on de face of the earth we don't have to fool ourselves by sayin' it's some sort of holy crusade or just fairness if we get our chance finally to kick the hell out of somebody else for a change. . . .

FIRST BROTHER   Teach, Brother.

SECOND BROTHER   *That's right! Bring it on down front, Brother!*

FAT SISTER   Right! . . . We's de most honest folks . . . history proves dat.

BOSS BROTHER   *(After hesitation)* Now, Brothers and mah good Sisters, now are we really honest? *(Before* HE *is answered)* Nawh, we are no more honest den other humans, for dishonesty is a human trait. *Ain't it!* And ain't we humans?

VOICES   *That's right! That's right! We's human, ain't we's!*

YOUNG SISTER   Teach, teach, teach, Brother.

With the white handkerchief at his forehead, the SPEAKER *stares out at the* NEW MAN *as* HE *raises his eyes from the floor. The* VISITOR *begins trembling.*

BOSS BROTHER   *(Winks, speaks)* The reason we's don't have to worry 'bout honesty is because dis ain't our society no way and what's ain't yours you don't have to care about no way. . . .

LOUD BROTHER   *(Stands in his chair, exhorting* BOSS BROTHER*)* That's right! That's right! What we's here fo is to get the facts, the truth and nothin' but!

FIRST BROTHER   Shut up, man, let Boss Brother talk!

SECOND BROTHER   Yeah, let us hear the word.

LOUD BROTHER *glares about the stage and takes his seat.* BOSS
BROTHER *'s eyes scan the stage and the audience like a hypnotist's
and the* VISITOR *shows distress.*

BOSS BROTHER   *(Confidentially)* Now let me tell you something you
might not have guessed before. You might not have known it
but dis ain't America in the sixties.

LOUD BROTHER   What you say, Brother?

BOSS BROTHER   *You wanted the truth, so I'm tellin' you that dis ain't
America you's in . . . right?*

FIRST BROTHER   That's what you said, Brother. That's what you said.

BOSS BROTHER   Yaasss . . . now this is really Germany . . . the
Germany of the late twenties and thirties . . . right?

LOUD BROTHER   Nawh, Brother, nawh, man. We ain't gonna go fo
dat.

BOSS BROTHER   *(Disarmingly)* But, Brother, you want the truth, so
I am confessing dat I'm Hitler . . . right?

VOICES   *No! No! We ain't goin' fo dat!*

BOSS BROTHER   Ain't I's Hitler?

LOUD BROTHER   *(Smugly)* Nawh, yawh not no Hitler.

FAT SISTER   Maybe he's tellin' the truth. I always wondered what
happened to Hitler.

VISITOR   *(Rises and challenges* BOSS BROTHER*)* Yawhl jivin'
. . . yawhl shuckin'.

With a flick of his handkerchief BOSS BROTHER *slams the* VISITOR
back into his seat. As the lights dim momentarily, BOSS BROTHER

*dons a Storm Trooper's jacket and applies a Hitler moustache as
the* BROTHERS *and* SISTERS *placidly look on.*

BOSS BROTHER   And I told everyone I had a book coming out
. . . you don't know whether I have a book coming out . . . right?

VOICES   *Right!*

BOSS BROTHER   *(Straight arm salute) Sing right!*

VOICES   *Right!!!*

BOSS BROTHER   *(Strong dialect)* Sho nuf!

The VISITOR *whimpers and trembles, but his sounds are ignored.*

Ha ha ha . . . but Comrades, I am really Marx . . . right?

LOUD BROTHER   *(Dismayed)* Wrong!

BOSS BROTHER   *Sing right!!!*

VOICES   *Wrong!!!*

BOSS BROTHER   *(Rejoicing) Yawhl right? Brothers . . . ha ha ha*
. . . For I don't really knows that dere are only nine card-carryin'
members in the L.A. cell . . . do I's . . . or are dere ten . . . or
two hundred and fifty-eight?

The light on the SPEAKER *becomes hazy and waxes and wanes
as it changes hue.*

LOUD BROTHER   *(Pointing) Yawhl hear dat? . . . He's one of dem reds!*

BOSS BROTHER   *Wouldn't yawhl want to be a first class Communist
stead of a second class citizen?*

FIRST BROTHER   Nawhl.

SECOND BROTHER Yeah, man.

VOICES *(In flurries among themselves)* He said first class.

LOUD BROTHER I don't want ta be no mahthafukkin Communist.
. . . I's a good American.

YOUNG SISTER Shut up, Tom!

BOSS BROTHER Don't intimidate the young man . . . and get ahold
of yourselves, folks . . . cause I got news for you. Now what's our
password?

VOICES *Illogic!*

BOSS BROTHER *Yaaasss . . . children . . .* and fo dat I'll confess dat
I'm really an imposter . . . I's really Malcolm X . . . *bloods*
. . . (BOSS BROTHER *has removed his uniform and wig and puts
on horn-rimmed glasses and wipes his shaven head)*

SPIRIT OF MALCOLM X *(HE stands from his seat in the middle of the
audience and heads for the stage) That's an outright slanderous
lie put in your mouth by blue-eyed white devils! (The SPIRIT is
dressed in black suit and red tie)* I'm Malcolm X!

ALL *the* BROTHERS *stand to block the* INVADER *who rushes down
the center aisle through the* BROTHERS *and* SISTERS *who were
sitting in the front seats but who rise and give the* APPARITION
chase. The SPIRIT *leaps upon the stage. The* BROTHERS *on stage
encircle it as* BOSS BROTHER *tries to crawl under his podium, and
the* VISITOR *huddles within the ranks of* WOMEN *who scream
encouragement to the* BROTHERS.

LOUD BROTHER *(Rushes up to the* SPIRIT *but remains out of reach)*
I's a killer, a mangler, a mad dog when I's gets started. I's so bad
I's have to hold myself back. *(Shakes his fist)* You better be
careful, boy!

The BROTHERS *have taken karate stances.* LOUD BROTHER *finally goes back to the* CROWD *and pushes* FIRST BROTHER *within the* SPIRIT*'s reach. The* SPIRIT *breaks* FIRST BROTHER*'s neck, backbone and hipbone with a nifty judo chop, and a terrific brawl ensues wherein the* SPIRIT *disables over half of the* BROTHERS *before* HE *is dragged outside.*

LOUD BROTHER   *(From the sidelines)* Liar.

FIRST BROTHER   *(Being mauled)* Peace, Brother.

SECOND BROTHER   *(Gets in a lick)* Fraud.

SPIRIT   *(Retaliates)* Take that, Brother.

YOUNG SISTER   *(In* CROWD*)* Mahthafukker!

VOICES   Teach da truth!

LOUD BROTHER   *(To audience as the* SPIRIT *is taken off)* He better not come back or I'll whup him so bad his mama won't take him in.

BOSS BROTHER   *(Peers from his hiding place and sees that all is clear)* I'm glad that cowardly dog is gone. *(*HE *has rows of ribbons displayed upon his chest)* To attempt to smear my good name . . . the idea.

FIRST BROTHER   *(Returns in bandages and on crutches)* Hush up *(To boasting* BROTHERS*)* so we can hear de word.

SECOND BROTHER   Yeah, hush on up!

BOSS BROTHER   See, now that order has been gotten at the expense of a few, I can positively say that I am Lenin, right, for he came before Stalin, so I am my own Second Coming, right?

FAT SISTER   Woweee . . . listen to him . . . he knows everybody.

YOUNG SISTER   Then he must be everybody!

The VISITOR *moans and* MANY HEADS *turn.*

OLD SISTER   *(To* BOSS BROTHER*)* Hush up yo lyin' mouf, man!

BOSS BROTHER   *(In time with a blinding flash of light)* But, Sister, ain't you never seen me befo? . . .

An explosion takes place under the SPEAKER*'s platform, causing a cloud to rise about him.*

OLD SISTER   *(Cowering)* Nawh . . . I ain't never seen no nothin' like you before.

The spot on BOSS BROTHER *dims gradually and the one on the likeness of The Serene Man brightens.*

BOSS BROTHER   Well, I've been away for quite some time, honey. You see, I's really the Wandering Jew.

LOUD BROTHER   The Wandering Who?

BOSS BROTHER   *(As lights change color)* Don't yawhl knows I's Martin Luther, Butterbeans without Susie. That I's Uncle Tom, Fred Schwarz, Emperor Goldwater, Lumumba, Castro, all the L.B.J.'s, Lincoln Rockwell, the Birds' Turds resurrected . . . chickenshit, ya hip?

LOUD BROTHER   Teach, Brother.

FIRST BROTHER   *That's right!*

SECOND BROTHER   Sho nuf . . . dat's where it's at.

BOSS BROTHER   And in all my glory . . . I's de greatest.

LOUD BROTHER   *(Staggering and screaming) That's right!*

YOUNG SISTER   *(Emotionally)* Teach, Brother . . . speak the Word, the Word, the Word!

BOSS BROTHER   Very well, I'll give you more, everything and whatever you wish to hear.

FIRST BROTHER   Give it to us, Brother.

YOUNG SISTER   Teach . . . teach . . . teach, Brother.

FAT SISTER   The Word, the Word, the Word.

All lights blacken except for the spot focused upon the picture of The Serene Man.

SERENE MAN   *(Voice of* BOSS BROTHER*)* I's de greatest. . . . I's de one and only who will hip ya to dis, Brothers! There's ah messiah on every corner! . . . 'N we're all out here to fuck ya . . . Brothers!

LOUD BROTHER   *(As lights go up) The truth! The final truth! (*HE *throws back his head and wails)*

FAT SISTER   *(Frenzied ecstasy)* Aaaa wooo ouwwalll weesss wa booogie blues in de alley soul so much soul so soulful, lawdy, yes, indeedy, yawhl.

BOSS BROTHER   *(Appears in his original clothes)* Now, yawhl knows dat I's goin' to take ov'va, so let me tell ya how's I's goin' to do it so you can help me. (HE *walks to the blackboard and in bright chalk writes large letters, then reads them aloud) Dialect determinism . . . yawhl!*

Rustles stir within the BROTHERS*' and* SISTERS*' ranks, and grunts of cleared throats are mingled with the squawks of parrots and farts of zebras.*

FIRST BROTHER   Dialect . . . what's dat?

SECOND BROTHER   Ummmmmmmm? ? . . .

BOSS BROTHER   *Remember those words, Brother.*

VOICES   We'll remember.

BOSS BROTHER   Now, to bind us closer together we needs a martyr.

LOUD BROTHER   *Yeah, dat's what we needs is a martyr!*

FIRST BROTHER   *(To* LOUD BROTHER*)* Say, what's dat?

> *Eyes search throughout the room, under seats, in pockets and purses, to the* VISITOR *drying his eyes.* HE *shakes his head and stares toward* YOUNG SISTER *who stands straightening her hose.* SHE *looks charming in her shift.*

YOUNG SISTER   *(Sees all eyes upon her)* Don't look at me *(Ridicules)* . . . Brothers and Sisters . . . *(*SHE *turns and stares at* BOSS BROTHER*)*

BOSS BROTHER   *(Finds all eyes upon him) Right!*

VOICES   *Right!!!*

> *The* BROTHERS *and* SISTERS *surge upon the stage. The* VISITOR, *the* YOUNG SISTER *and the* DOORMAN *remain in their places.*

BOSS BROTHER   *(Salutes as* HE *is stomped) Sing right!!!*

VOICES   *(The* GROUP *tears at* BOSS BROTHER *like carrion) Right!!!*

LOUD BROTHER   I'll get the rope.

> HE *rushes to the* DOORMAN *who hands him the rope and returns to the* MOB. *After* LOUD BROTHER *receives the rope, the* VISITOR *accepts his personal items.* HE *talks in a whisper to the* YOUNG SISTER *who has wandered over and is giggling.*

DOORMAN   Come again, Brother.

VISITOR   I'll try.

> *Sound of the* MOB *as* THEY *part to show* LOUD BROTHER *garroting* BOSS BROTHER.

DOORMAN   Never seen my people in such high spirits. Well, good night, Brother. Good night, Sister. Peace be with you. *(*HE *about-faces and begins his patrol)*

VISITOR   *(With* YOUNG SISTER *on his arm)* And Peace remain with you . . . Brother. *(*HE *looks at the image of The Serene Man and at the* DOORMAN*'s back, then leads* YOUNG SISTER *away)*

SANIBEL AND CAPTIVA
A Radio Play
Megan Terry

For Renee Kaplan

Sanibel and Captiva is written, as a radio play must be, mainly for the ear (though I can imagine it staged beautifully). A wonderful piece of chamber music for two voices, a litany of middle America, chillingly enveloped in an aura of death. A husband and wife are fishing together, fishing for human contact and spiritual fulfillment, fishing for each other and for a society in which they can feel at home. Such is Megan Terry's precision and knowledge of her archetypal people that the play's symbolism only strengthens its validity as a realistic study.

CHARACTERS

BUD
ESTHER

SETTING: An island off the coast of Florida in the Gulf of Mexico. A retired couple, BUD and ESTHER, are fishing in the surf.

SOUND: *Surf, tropical birds, shells being washed up against other shells. A dog barks.*

BUD   Is anyone coming?

ESTHER   No.

BUD   The dog barked.

ESTHER   Birds.

SOUND: *Gulls.*

BUD   Well, someone might be coming.

ESTHER   No.

BUD   The dog barked.

ESTHER   Nobody's coming.

BUD   The dog barked. *(Pause)* Somebody might be coming.

ESTHER   Nobody's coming.

BUD   I wish they'd come.

ESTHER   They will.

BUD   When?

ESTHER   Sunday.

BUD   Sunday?

ESTHER   The kids might come.

BUD   Do you think so?

ESTHER   Yes. Sunday the kids will come.

BUD   I hope so.

ESTHER   They will.

BUD   They caught their limit?

ESTHER   Lake Chelan is full of trout this year.

BUD   Thank God. Been a long time since you could catch your limit.

ESTHER   The kids will come. *(Pause)*

BUD   Too bad Jim hasn't had enough work.

ESTHER   Well, you know how it is in winter. The Teamsters can't always come up with a job.

BUD   But you'd think after all these years he'd be first one for the . . .

ESTHER   It's not at all like that.

BUD   I don't understand. . . .

ESTHER   Well, how could you. . . .

SOUND: *A large wave breaks against the shell banks.*

BUD   I want some blackberries. . . .

ESTHER   They don't grow around here anymore. I'd trade my left arm for a pint of tart blackberries.

BUD   I don't want to hear about it.

ESTHER   Yes, you do.

BUD   I don't want to hear about . . .

ESTHER   You like to hear . . .

BUD   I don't want to hear about things that don't grow anymore.

ESTHER   You do. It makes you cry.

BUD   Hate to cry.

ESTHER   You like to hear about things that make you cry.

BUD   Washes out the eyes.

ESTHER   Cleans the brain too. Get a bite?

BUD   Nibbles.

ESTHER   It's good to be here. Especially when the sun starts to go down.

BUD   It's nice to see color in the sky.

ESTHER   What makes it?

BUD   The color?

ESTHER   What makes the color?

BUD   Well, the air, and your eyes have a lot to do with it I think.

ESTHER   I think you've got a fish, Bud.

BUD   Shhhh. . . .

ESTHER   I see the end of your rod. . . .

BUD   Let me alone. . . .

ESTHER   But it's . . .

BUD   Quiet. . . .

ESTHER   Reel it in.

SOUND: *Surf and gulls.*

BUD   No, not yet . . . he's got to swallow the bait.

ESTHER   But your rod's bent nearly double.

BUD   It's wobbling . . . if I'm not patient . . . I'll . . .

ESTHER   Bud, reel in the line.

BUD   Esther . . .

ESTHER   I can't stand it.

BUD   Reel in your own line.

ESTHER   Nothing's biting.

BUD   Leave me alone, I know what I'm doing.

ESTHER   I want a snapper tonight.

BUD   If I don't get one, I'll buy you a pompano.

ESTHER   I'd rather have our own.

BUD   Leave me alone.

ESTHER   I didn't say anything.

BUD   I'm playing him out.

ESTHER   Well, do what you want. I haven't said anything.

BUD   I can't whip up the end of the rod just for a nibble. I have to let him swallow the bait, because, if it's a trout, and I jerk up the line, then the hook will pull right out of his mouth. Sea trout have the tenderest mouths in the world. Got a feeling a snook's circling. Do you think I could pull in a snook?

ESTHER   I'll give you a hand.

BUD   Snook can be heavy.

ESTHER   But with two of us . . .

BUD   It's not the right time of year.

ESTHER   It might be a baby snook.

BUD   Wouldn't be the first time.

   SOUND: *Wings flapping.*

ESTHER   Hey, what's that bird?

BUD   Ibetz. . . .

SOUND: *Mynahs chattering.*

Mynahs cussing us out right and left.

ESTHER   You know what I'd like to drink?

BUD   Yes.

ESTHER   A scotch sour.

BUD   Me too.

ESTHER   I'll run up to the house and make us one.

BUD   I'll go with you.

ESTHER   Angel.

BUD   Sweetheart.

ESTHER   Brother.

BUD   Darling.

ESTHER   Why is it we have so much for one another?

BUD   Don't ask.

ESTHER   Hold me.

BUD   Yes. Kiss?

ESTHER   Yes.

BUD   It's good.

ESTHER   Of course.

BUD   It's really good.

ESTHER   Oh, my. Hold me tighter.

SOUND: *A car approaches.*

BUD   The car.

ESTHER   The kids?

BUD   Might be them.

ESTHER   Well, we wanted them to come.

BUD   Now?

ESTHER   Well, they're here.

BUD   Maybe we could tell them to come again next week.

ESTHER   But they drove five hundred miles.

BUD   We don't feel like this that often.

ESTHER   We can't send them away.

BUD   Why not?

ESTHER   We can't.

BUD   We could.

ESTHER   We could pretend we weren't at home.

BUD   Nonsense, they're our kids.

ESTHER   Well, we could say we're not well.

BUD   We're not so well, but the fact is, we haven't been so marvelously well in such a long time. They'll have to wait.

ESTHER   Your rod is bent double, if you don't pull it in I'm going to get upset.

BUD   I'm playing him. I know it's bent double. I'm playing him, Esther. Give me the benefit of the doubt, please. I've been fishing five years longer than you. I know when and how to bring in a red fish. I have to let the rod bend double, before I can set the hook; otherwise he'll let it go. Be patient.

ESTHER   Bud, I don't know how to tell you this, but some of the people want you to go away for awhile.

SOUND: *Mynahs laughing.*

BUD   But I've been away.

ESTHER   They want you to leave here.

BUD   Who told you?

ESTHER   They formed a delegation and they met with me yesterday at lunch.

BUD   While I slept?

ESTHER   No, you were watching the turkey buzzards.

BUD   At the Sanctuary.

ESTHER   No, it was at the old Bailey place. You were up in the tower.

BUD   Did I get any good pictures?

ESTHER   They're being developed.

BUD   I hope I had my telephoto lens on.

ESTHER   They sent this delegation.

BUD   What did you have for lunch?

ESTHER   Caesar salad and planters punch.

BUD   Meyers rum?

ESTHER   That's what I asked for.

BUD   I saw ten thousand sparrows on the walk back home. They flew in every direction. A circus. It was a sparrow circus. I've never seen anything like it. It was like the locusts in the China picture. . . .

ESTHER   *The Good Earth.* . . .

BUD   Yes . . . it was like in *The Good Earth.* These sparrows darting and falling and recovering and they were so thick I could barely make out if the sky was blue or cloudy.

SOUND: *A car approaches.*

BUD   It's an Olds.

ESTHER   The kids have been planning to come down here for a long time.

BUD   I was up all night again.

ESTHER   No you weren't.

BUD   I know if I was up all night. I couldn't sleep.

ESTHER   You just think you couldn't. I heard you snoring.

BUD   Only a minute. Woke myself up. Couldn't get back to sleep. Are they here yet?

ESTHER   I heard a car.

SOUND: *Surf and gulls.*

BUD   Sweetheart?

ESTHER   Yes. . . .

BUD   Sweetheart?

ESTHER   Yes. . . .

BUD   Sweetheart.

ESTHER   They came to me and asked me to tell you that you upset them when you go down to the club.

BUD   Me?

ESTHER   They seem to think you put them off their game.

BUD   But I don't say a word. I smile and I watch. . . . I hardly ever speak. I nod and discuss the weather, and I tell how many fish I caught. How could I put them off their game? I only stay an hour or two, I don't even suggest which card to play, even when I can see how they could have taken another trick.

ESTHER   I don't know how to tell you this. I told them they should take it up with you personally.

BUD   Well, they should.

ESTHER   I didn't want to be the one to have to tell you. After all, it has nothing to do with me.

BUD How could I put them off their game? I don't even play their game.

ESTHER Here's the letter from the club president.

BUD I thought he spoke to you.

ESTHER He did. He told me to tear up the letter. He couldn't seem to remember if he'd mailed it. He said that he wrote you three letters, he thought, but he couldn't remember mailing them, and anyway, he said that it would be better if he spoke, because no matter how he tried to write it, he couldn't say what it was that you did that bothered the other club members.

BUD Read me the letter.

ESTHER Well, here it is.

BUD When did he mail it?

ESTHER Let me see, the postmark is February 12, P.M.

BUD Lincoln's Birthday?

ESTHER I think so.

BUD That was yesterday.

ESTHER I think so.

BUD Did we observe it?

ESTHER We didn't know about it.

BUD I guess we didn't know about it till today.

SOUND: *A car approaches.*

BUD   I'd swear it's an Oldsmobile.

ESTHER   I can't tell one car from another.

BUD   Used to love to watch the machines go by when I was younger. I know every machine that was ever made. Could draw you a picture of any one of them—that is, if I could draw, but I got the picture plain as day in my head. I could tell you every marking and every curve and even the right colors of the models according to their price range.

SOUND: *Gulls wheeling—a fish jumps.*

ESTHER   Your line.

BUD   What, what?

ESTHER   Your line. He hit it again. Look at the tip.

BUD   Forty bites. I've had forty bites.

ESTHER   Set the hook.

BUD   Not so fast.

ESTHER   We need dinner.

BUD   Not so fast.

ESTHER   I'm longing for fresh fish.

BUD   Hold your horses.

ESTHER   Reel him in.

BUD   It's just a little fellow eating around the edges of the shrimp.

ESTHER   Flip the tip. Get him in.

BUD   It won't do any good.

ESTHER   I can't bear the suspense.

BUD   Reel in your own line.

ESTHER   Nothing's happening.

BUD   I'll bet you're skunked.

ESTHER   Nothing's there.

BUD   I'll bet you're clean out of bait.

ESTHER   How do you know?

BUD   You haven't had a nibble in five minutes.

ESTHER   There he goes again. Oh, set the hook, set the hook.

BUD   Be patient. We've been fishing together for forty years, and you're getting less patient. Why, you used to sit with me all day, and never say a word except pass the salt. That's why I married you. I didn't have to talk to you—you always seemed to know what I was thinking, and me, you.

ESTHER   You knew what I was thinking?

BUD   I always knew what you were thinking.

ESTHER   Do you know?

BUD   What?

ESTHER   Do you always know what I'm thinking now?

BUD   Only when I look at you.

ESTHER I had a premonition when he came to the door.

BUD Why wasn't I at home?

ESTHER You were watching the turkey buzzards.

BUD Got some good pictures of 'em too. God they love to fly. They hover and . . .

ESTHER They love to eat, that's why they look like that in the sky.

BUD But the way they hang there in the air . . .

ESTHER Looking for food, that's what makes 'em look like that.

BUD But the way they glide. . . .

ESTHER Watching for a cripple to gobble, that's why they glide like that. . . .

BUD I like to watch them.

ESTHER They're watching you.

BUD I can feel him again.

ESTHER Set the hook.

BUD Too soon.

ESTHER Set the hook.

BUD No, I like to feel him there. I'm waiting. I'm going to land you the biggest snook for this time of year you ever saw. It's nothing to catch a snook in June. But now. Watch out. I'm going to land a ten pound snook, and then let them draw up their chairs and ask what I used for bait.

ESTHER   That's what I wanted to tell you about.

BUD   What's that?

ESTHER   They want you to stay away for a while, Bud. They don't want you coming around the club for a while.

SOUND: *Mynahs chattering and calling.*

BUD   I was up all night again, Esther.

ESTHER   Not again.

BUD   Couldn't get to sleep.

ESTHER   You just think you didn't sleep.

BUD   I know I didn't sleep. I can tell you everything I was thinking about the whole night long.

ESTHER   So can I. It's the same things you've been thinking about any night you were up.

BUD   I don't feel as tired as I was afraid I'd be. Want to catch you that snook. I know how much you like snook broiled in butter and lemon fresh from the Gulf.

ESTHER   I like it, I really do like it. Better than steak to me.

BUD   I think you were an Indian princess in your former life.

ESTHER   I suppose I was.

BUD   Never did know anyone to enjoy fish as much as you.

ESTHER   I could live on it. I could eat snook or snapper every day of my life and never tire of it.

BUD   I'm gonna get you a fresh one today.

ESTHER   They haven't been running.

BUD   Fishing is a matter of confidence. I know I'll catch one today. Like last week, I just didn't feel lucky. I didn't have a grasp on the pole, I didn't have confidence in the tide. And I didn't catch much of anything but some whiting and ladyfish. Today is something else. I know I'm gonna get you one.

SOUND: *Surf and a light wind. A dog barks.*

ESTHER   I'm going to tear up the letter.

BUD   No.

ESTHER   Yes, I'm going to tear it up. It's too hurtful—unjust.

BUD   If that's the way they feel about me, then I should know what it is.

ESTHER   No, I think I'll tear it up.

BUD   I'd just as soon face it. Give it to me.

ESTHER   No, it's entirely unjust. You didn't have any control in the project and they have overlooked that fact.

BUD   I made some money out of it, that's what's sticking in their craws.

ESTHER   Could be.

BUD   I tried. I tried every way I knew to get them all a piece of it, but I was only one of five. The other four blackballed my friends. But it's me gets the blame.

ESTHER   They feel they helped you find the land.

BUD   Well, they did. But it was me figured out the way to develop it, and get the backing to make the project come true. Every lot has been sold. Every one a waterfront property; every one with his own dock and fishing pier. I tried to get my friends in on it, but they didn't want to take the initial risk. Now I made a little change out of it, and they want to get even with me. I voted for them, the other four men voted no. What could I do? Are they angry at the ones voted against them? No, it's me. You're right, it is hurtful. I don't want to think about it. Do they want to throw me out of the club?

ESTHER   They want to ban you for a while.

BUD   Ban me?

ESTHER   Yes, they don't want you to come around and watch the card games for six weeks.

BUD   Six weeks. Where'd they get six weeks?

ESTHER   The president feels that if they sentence you to six weeks of not coming around the club, it will kind of even the score, and then the rest of them will go on with you.

BUD   I helped build the club. I helped get it established.

ESTHER   Well, the new members feel crowded, he said.

BUD   The new members! It's really enough to make a guy want to quit something, no matter how much he loved it in the start, when the newest members carry the most weight.

ESTHER   There are a lot of them. I guess they can outvote.

SOUND: *Mynahs laughing.*

BUD   I bet it isn't the new members. What would the new members want with hurting me? They don't know me well enough to want to hurt me. It's the oldtimers feel I'm out of touch with them. That's what they want. They want to hurt me. They want to really hurt me. Didn't know I had that kind of power.

SOUND: *A car goes by very fast.*

ESTHER   I think I'll tear it up.

BUD   No, you'll do nothing of the kind. I'm going to paste it on the bathroom mirror. I want to be reminded every day how vengeful people are with nothing but emotion to back them up. They have the facts all wrong. They've assumed I'm against them when there was nobody more *for* them. I don't control the world. I can't manage every event. They've turned on me—I, who set them up in the first place. They learned a lot about business and land development in their association with me. They're all better fixed now, and smarter than when we started. Had a friend in the old days, used to say there's no justice. I take my hat off to you, Roger. Had to live a long time to say you're right.

SOUND: *Huge waves begin to break on the shore.*

BUD   Get back out of the tide, Esther.

ESTHER   It feels good around my ankles.

BUD   Get back out, I say. Look. Look there.

ESTHER   Fins?

BUD   Sharks.

ESTHER   Porpoise.

BUD   Don't take a chance.

ESTHER   That's not a shark.

BUD   There's two of 'em. Get back, Esther, they're feeding four feet from shore. They could dash in and snap! You'd pull back a stump instead of a leg.

ESTHER   Nonsense. That's not a shark.

BUD   He came up just three feet from shoreline. They can roll on their bellies and pretend to be flounder. Last summer a little girl had her arm bitten off at the shoulder by one of them devils.

ESTHER   *(Laughing)* It's a porpoise.

BUD   Want to bet?

ESTHER   I don't want to bet. I like the tide washing over my legs.

BUD   Your slacks are getting wet, too.

ESTHER   I don't care. All my life I wanted to be able to stand in the water and fish and it's warm enough here. Look at the sunset.

BUD   Supposed to go down at six fifty-five. It's right on schedule. Are you going to get out of the drink or am I going to throw you over my shoulder?

ESTHER   You been here long enough to tell a shark fin from a porpoise. Look how they roll and play with one another. No shark ever does like that.

BUD   Get out of the water. Now. I'm going to get out the fish book and we'll settle it. I don't want to take no chances with you, sweetheart.

ESTHER   What?

BUD   Sweetheart.

ESTHER   What. . . .

BUD   Sweetheart.

ESTHER   What. . . .

BUD   Sweetheart, now do like I ask, just to please me. Get out of the water. Don't take a chance.

ESTHER   All right.

BUD   Thank you.

SOUND: *A car in the distance.*

BUD   The kids must have had to drive night and day.

ESTHER   Jim loves to drive.

BUD   He never gets enough rest.

ESTHER   They keep him on the go.

BUD   He's been a go-getter for them.

ESTHER   They use him up.

BUD   He doesn't know how to ration himself out.

ESTHER   I can't wait to see him.

BUD   Are they bringing the children?

ESTHER   All but Susan. She's training for the swimming team.

BUD   She could swim here.

ESTHER   She has to work with her coach.

BUD   She seems so young to spend so many hours going around and about in a pool.

ESTHER   She's like her father.

BUD   Why'd they want to drive down here?

ESTHER   You know Jim loves to drive.

BUD   He should have taken the plane and saved up on himself.

ESTHER   He can't stand to have anyone else doing the driving.

BUD   Should have taken the plane. I'd have advanced him the money. I'm going over to the club, and I'm going to have a talk with all of them and get the whole thing out in the open.

ESTHER   That's a good idea.

BUD   It's the only thing to do. But if I do do that? . . . Read me the letter. But if they are so hurt with me, maybe they *should* have a chance to get even.

ESTHER   And let them get away with hurting you?

BUD   I can stand it better than they can. Maybe if they do bar me from the club for a while, it'll satisfy their hurts and then when I do go back, we can all start over with a clean slate.

ESTHER   They'll just be laughing up their sleeves at you. You should go there and tell them off and quit.

BUD   But I helped start the club.

ESTHER   You can start another.

BUD   It's meant a lot to me.

ESTHER You give them too much.

BUD Well, it has meant a lot to me, can't deny it.

ESTHER You go over there and resign.

BUD Can't do that. Maybe I'll say nothing and never go back. Yes,
I think that's what I'll do. I'll keep quiet and I'll never go back.
Then what will they do with their anger? Yes. I think I'll keep
quiet and never go back. Do you have the letter?

ESTHER You never get mad enough.

BUD What good does it do?

ESTHER You just won't get mad.

BUD I'm not mad.

ESTHER You're hurt.

BUD No I'm not. Yes, yes of course, I am.

ESTHER And tomorrow you'll be depressed and you won't talk to me
for days.

BUD I won't be depressed.

ESTHER You can't help it.

BUD I won't be depressed. I'll take you to the Plantation for dinner.

ESTHER It's a pretty place, but they don't know how to cook.

BUD I'll catch you a snook today and I'll catch you a snapper
tomorrow. You know how to cook.

ESTHER Sweetheart.

BUD   Yes.

ESTHER   Sweetheart.

BUD   Hello.

SOUND: *Mynahs laughing, gulls screaming and complaining. The dog barks and a flock of gulls ascends.*

ESTHER   I dreamed about my sister again, Bud.

BUD   Been years since you've seen her.

ESTHER   Can't understand it. I don't think about her for months, and then I get such a dream. I nearly woke you.

BUD   I was awake. . . . I was awake all night. . . .

ESTHER   She wouldn't get me a doctor. I felt terribly ill. My period was two weeks overdue. I was frightened that I was pregnant, but I knew I hadn't slept with anyone. I didn't think I had, but I had fears that I had and blotted it out. I was so upset. I walked around day and night saying, Esther get the curse. Esther get the curse. Esther get the curse. Every hour I felt more bloated. Every time I went to the bathroom, I'd look down, hoping for the blood, but I always knew it wouldn't be there. I began to plan for an abortion, but I didn't know how. I thought I knew a lot, but when I was face to face with the possibility that something was growing inside me against my will, I couldn't believe it. But the *fact* that something was growing against my will comforted me in a strange way, because I really had nothing to do with it. And yet I knew I couldn't be pregnant. I've never done anything unplanned.

BUD   Read me the letter.

ESTHER   My sister was there and I asked her to get me the doctor. I wanted him to give me a shot to bring on menstruation.

BUD   Read me the letter. I'm ready to hear it now.

ESTHER   I begged my sister to get me the doctor. She hesitated and
waited and stalled and found a million things to do. I grew weak
and suddenly blood started to pour in spurts from my anus. The
bloat from my insides came out the wrong way. I thought I was
giving up my bones and my guts. I became paper-thin and shook
all over. It happened so fast. I thought, this is how it is to die.
Your body turns on you and everything comes out the wrong
way. I begged her to get the doctor, but I kept slipping in my
blood clots all over the floor. So much blood, I didn't know there
could be that much in a human body, all coming out the wrong
way. I begged her to get the doctor. She left for a minute and
when she came back she said the doctor wouldn't come. I said
I needed him.

BUD   Sweetheart.

ESTHER   She laughed and started to clean out her pocketbook. The
doctor doesn't waste his time on death you know, she said. He
said anyone who bled like that would be dead before he got to
the door and he had too much to do. Anyone who bled like that
was nearly dead anyway, so he wouldn't come. I didn't believe
she'd really gone to the doctor, but I was afraid she had.

SOUND: *A car approaches. The dog barks.*

BUD   I think it's a Chevrolet.

ESTHER   You always did love that white car.

BUD   Nothing ever happened to it except a flat tire.

ESTHER   It got us where we wanted to go.

BUD   You can say that again. Never had any trouble. The hum of
the motor—must be an Impala.

ESTHER   You can't hear anything in the new cars.

BUD   They're quiet as riding on a pin.

ESTHER   That's what I mean.

SOUND: *Mynahs calling.*

BUD   I probably should do it myself, but it's no fun. And yet, it's the only way. You can only do it yourself, and then there's nobody to blame but yourself, but it's mighty damn lonely to work like that.

ESTHER   Don't see why you'd want to please them anyway.

BUD   Give me your hand.

ESTHER   Not till you check your bait.

BUD   All right.

ESTHER   Reel in the line.

BUD   All right.

SOUND: *A spinning reel.*

ESTHER   There, I knew it.

BUD   Skunked.

ESTHER   Wha'd I tell you?

BUD   I thought sure that . . .

ESTHER   I'm putting on a whole shrimp for you this time.

BUD   They'll only gobble it.

ESTHER   Take a chance.

BUD   Don't use a whole shrimp. He won't last thirty seconds out there.

ESTHER   We'll see.

BUD   I tell you . . .

ESTHER   My mouth's watering. . . .

BUD   You'll see. It won't last thirty . . . How long did that last little bit you cast out go for?

SOUND: *Spinning reel casting out.*

ESTHER   We'll never know. You think you're magic. You think the fish will walk right out of the water into the fry pan, with nothing in between but your will power.

BUD   It won't last. . . .

ESTHER   We'll see. . . . Look there. Set the hook now! Your rod's bent double. Here, give it to me.

BUD   I did it. I got it. This is a big one. Weighs a ton. I can't lift the rod.

ESTHER   Walk backward. Walk backward up the beach. You'll lose him in the surf.

BUD   Sweetheart . . .

ESTHER   Let me hold you, you're shaking.

BUD   It won't stop. I can't stop shaking.

ESTHER   Pull the fish up the bank.

BUD   The pole is beating my hands. I can't hang on.

ESTHER   I've got you.

BUD   Beating like a devil against my hands.

ESTHER   Hang on.

BUD   I can't.

ESTHER   Hang on.

BUD   I'm trying.

ESTHER   Hang on.

BUD   I can't.

ESTHER   Hang on.

BUD   Take it.

ESTHER   Hang on.

BUD   Read me the letter.

ESTHER   I'm going to tear it up. He told me to tear it up.

BUD   I want to know what it said. I can face it.

ESTHER   Your legs gave out.

BUD   Read me the letter.

ESTHER   The kids should be here any minute.

BUD   I don't know why you still speak to your sister.

ESTHER   Why not?

BUD   She laughs at your feelings.

ESTHER   I know.

BUD   Why do you let yourself in for it?

ESTHER   Why don't you resign from the club?

SOUND: *A car approaches.*

ESTHER   I'm pregnant.

BUD   I hope it's a Lincoln.

ESTHER   Something's growing.

BUD   My favorite shape was always the Lincoln Continental of 1946.

ESTHER   If you wrap a cheesecloth around the lemon before you squeeze, no seeds drop in.

BUD   I'll write them a letter. They think they can write me a letter. Well, let me tell you the United States mails run both ways.

SOUND: *Gulls complaining.*

BUD   Sweetheart.

ESTHER   I brought you a scotch sour.

BUD   Never had anything to quench thirst so fast.

ESTHER   I had to clean the blood up off the floor.

BUD   Don't pay no attention.

ESTHER It took me longer than I thought.

BUD Don't make no nevermind.

ESTHER There were so many clumps. It wouldn't drain away.

BUD You did your best.

ESTHER I see the snout.

BUD Are you sure it's a fish?

ESTHER Mammals have to be thrown back. I had my heart set on snook.

BUD Better than salmon. Funny how your tastes change when you change your countryside. I always thought nothing could beat the taste of salmon.

ESTHER Cooked in milk with mayonnaise in the belly. Cooked in milk in the oven, forty-five minutes, then under the broiler for seven, that's the way to do it.

BUD Oh, could snook truly taste that good?

ESTHER Can you pull him over the surf? I'm going to give you a hand.

BUD I can do it.

ESTHER Can you see the snout?

BUD If he has lips . . .

ESTHER Scales?

BUD It's too early for snook. If I had a helicopter, I could see the whole island in a second.

ESTHER   The beach is filling with people. I hope they don't ask us what we're doing.

BUD   Makes a guy feel uncomfortable.

ESTHER   They just scratch in the sand for shells. We want something fresh.

SOUND: *Airplane.*

BUD   There goes the jet to New York. They're eating steak up there.

ESTHER   They can have it. I'm sorry it took me so long. I couldn't soak it up. I had to use the salad spoon. I didn't want you to come back to the cabin to that. But I couldn't help it.

BUD   Sweetheart . . .

ESTHER   I'll wade in and push him toward you.

BUD   No, he could flip you under, and what with the undertow . . .

ESTHER   Oh, the undertow. Oh, the undertow. What undertow? I been standing in the surf ever since we came to Florida, and haven't even been tipped.

BUD   The sand gives way with every wave.

ESTHER   I keep moving.

BUD   You don't pay enough attention. You get so set on that fish out there, you forget yourself.

ESTHER   But that's why I like it here.

BUD   Look at him fight. Look at that son of a gun jump. This is the meanest fish I ever hooked.

ESTHER   He's silver. He's . . . The stripe. It's the snook stripe. . . .

BUD   On the last flip, did you . . .

ESTHER   It's him, all right.

BUD   Oh.

ESTHER   Oh.

BUD   Sweetheart.

ESTHER   Oh.

SOUND: *A line snapping.*

BUD   *(A cry)* Sweetheart!

ESTHER   I saw it. I saw it snap in the air . . . so fast . . . so fast. . . .

BUD   Ah. . . . I moved so slowly backward up the beach, I was sure I . . .

ESTHER   Throw your line over to me and I'll tie on another rig.

BUD   Ahhh . . .

ESTHER   Don't matter.

BUD   Your mouth was watering. I wanted to get you a . . .

SOUND: *Mynahs laugh. Dog barks. Two spinning reels cast out. A car approaches.*

A QUICK NUT BREAD
TO MAKE YOUR MOUTH WATER
William M. Hoffman

An Improvisatory Play

For Joe Pichette, Michael Ravis,

Julia Willis

A Quick Nut Bread to Make Your Mouth Water is
wonderfully innovative in its mix of improvisation and
formal text; an exalted playful creation, always renewing
itself, gleaning the insights and desperations of young
people in a patient and sustained quest for spiritual peace.

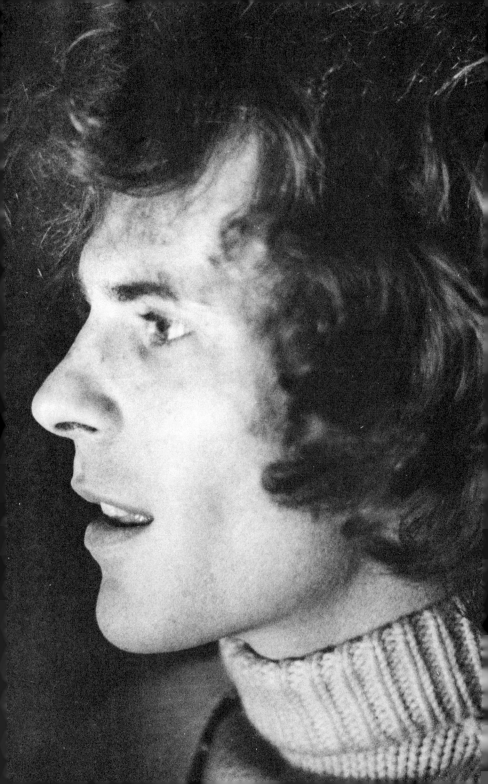

CHARACTERS

JOE: A cynical actor, about thirty, somewhat alcoholic.

JULIA: A pretty girl, somewhat plastic, about twenty, inexperienced but not dumb. She's studying to be an actress.

MICHAEL: Jesus hair, denim work shirt, levis, barefoot, sincere, warm, about nineteen.

VOICE of the AUTHOR.

LIGHT MAN

SCENE: JOE's apartment on St. Mark's Place, New York City, or any street of head shops, students, hippies, and revolutionaries in any American college town or city. The references in this play are to the New York scene; they might be changed when the play is done elsewhere.

MUSIC: Ideally, a small gospel, rock, or classical chamber group of from three to eight performers should accompany the play. If live music is not feasible, recorded music may be substituted and the lyrics included in the script disregarded. The musicians should be placed on stage with the actors and a warm, informal relationship between the two groups should be encouraged.

NOTE: The cast is dressed casually, and the production should look as casual as possible. Ideally, most of the play should seem improvised, which will take many rehearsals.

INGREDIENTS

JULIA's shopping bag—it is large—contains:
5-lb. bag of whole wheat flour
1/2 doz. eggs
16-oz. jar of honey
1 quart milk

1 small can walnuts
package of salt
1 can baking powder
small jar of vegetable oil
mixing bowls—big, medium, small
3 glasses
measuring spoons
measuring cup
mixing spoons
baking pan—about 6×10×3
bread recipe
1 cap-pistol set, including holster, belt, and caps
paperback copy of *The Upanishads*
3 aprons—one black, one white, one red
2 sets of finger cymbals

PROLOGUE

The only pieces on stage as the audience enters are a large table or counter covered by a bright tablecloth, center stage, and a large shopping bag, stage right. When the audience has been seated there is a blackout. The cast and musicians enter. JOE *sits on the floor center stage in front of the table;* JULIA *sits to the right of the table and* MICHAEL *to the left. About forty to fifty slides of people's eyes—the eyes of adults, children, old people, the eyes of people of all races and both sexes, just their eyes—are projected. As the last slide is projected, the taped sound of a type-writer is heard. Then:*

VOICE   This is the author speaking. This introduction was written at 2:30 in the morning after a day of the usual mixture of joy, madness, sorrow, and pleasure. The author was sitting at his desk —actually, he *is* sitting at his desk—as he types these words. His hands are trembling. He has just lit a cigarette. He takes a sip of coffee from a glazed earthenware cup. He types: "I AM." And so here he is, folks, here I am. And then he-I takes a sip,

oh, yes, he-I—every letter, every sound, is a doorway, friend, every second of time is a mirror. And now I, no longer he or he-I, and now I write and now I say: *"There is nothing else but consciousness."*
I think: I've invited other people to say my words. I think of the actor saying these words now to you. Now to you. *Now to you.* Who is this man saying my words? Who is this man you are listening to? Whom is this man saying my words to? Who are you sitting out there in the dark? I think of the man making believe he is Joe, making believe he is a Joe type of man, sitting out there in the dark in front of you also in the dark. In the dark corner of the room my black cat Christine is playing in the dark. . . .
I think—and now I say with my Olympia portable typewriter, with the hands of some quick union typesetter, with an Ampex tape recorder and Scotch recording tape, with the voice of a stranger, now I say: Light Man, put a small spot on the face of the man playing Joe . . .

Pin spot on JOE*'s face.*

. . . and when that is done, Joe, look at the audience.

JOE *performs this action and the following ones.*

Then, Joe, close your eyes and smile. . . . Now open your eyes and look at the audience again. Look up to heaven. . . . Bring your eyes back to earth. . . . Close them. . . . Open your eyes and say your lines—oh, Joe, one second, please.

JOE *looks a little startled.*

Julia and Michael, whoever you are, will you do the same with your eyes before you say your first lines, which by now you'll be able to do well, since by this time, this very second—oh, that second's passed—you'll probably have had two weeks to practice. Click. *(Tape goes off)*

JOE Hello out there, friend. Where are you right now? What are you thinking about? Sh, don't tell me. Let me guess. Are you thinking about the words I just said, or the words on the tape? Are you thinking about the words that will follow or the actions? I'll tell you the actions: we just show you how to make bread.

Pin spot on JULIA. SHE *performs the eye actions.*

JULIA Hello out there, friend. Where are you right now? Have you just had a drink? Does alcohol make you feel emotional? Are you into feelings? What does it feel like? Does it feel like pleasure? Does it feel like pain? Does it feel like love? Does it feel like hate? Does it feel just so-so? Whatever it feels like I hope it feels *good.*

Pin spot on MICHAEL. *Eye actions.*

MICHAEL Hello out there, friend. Where are you right now? Are you tripping? Hello, *it's so good!* Are you stoned on grass and into the details of the light in my hair *(Slowly shakes his long hair)* or the trembling of my hand as I extend my arm? *(HE extends his arm toward the audience)* Right now. Right now.

JOE Where are you right now? Are you speeding and *(Talking like a speed freak)* aware of the infinite number of concepts the mind is capable of producing one by one, all connected, wow!, the jewelled spiderweb of concepts and metaconcepts?

JULIA Are you in love? Have you come here with the person you're in love with? Is he sitting next to you? Is she right by you? He's just sittin' there next to you in the dark and you can put your arm around him, or she can take your hand. Oh, we *know* how it is.

The following quickly:

MICHAEL Are you confused?

JOE   Does your life lack meaning?

JULIA   Are you miserable?

JOE   Are you seeing a shrink?

MICHAEL   Have you tried encounter therapy?

JOE   Health foods?

MICHAEL   Communes?

JULIA   Are you into change within the system?

JOE   Liberation?

MICHAEL   Are you into revolution?

JOE   Do you chant "Nam-myo-ho-renge-kyo?" *(HE chants briefly)*

MICHAEL   Or "Hare Krishna?" *(HE chants briefly)*

JULIA   Are you a witch?

MICHAEL   Are you a criminal?

JULIA   Are you a murderer? Hello there, you who end lives.

JOE   Are you hungry? If you're hungry, we have bread for you later.

JULIA   We baked it this morning.

MICHAEL   Tonight we're making the dough for tomorrow's show.

JOE   Are you young? Does She happen to you in spurts—like continuous orgasms?

MICHAEL   Does She surprise you in Her variety?

JULIA Are you older? Have you learned the trick of sitting back and watching Her performance?

JOE Well, whatever your age, whoever you are: I tell you She

JULIA must be seen through

MICHAEL thick and thin—

JOE She's so pretty. Whoever you are

ALL *Hello!*

MUSICIANS *(Sing)*

> Hello, hello,
> It's mighty fine to see you.
> Hello, hello,
> We're glad that you're here.
> Howdy, howdy,
> How's it feel to be you?
> Howdy, howdy,
> You've nothing to fear.
> Hello, hello,
> We hope you enjoy us.
> Hello, hello,
> We're happy you've come.
> Hello, hello,
> Hello, hello.

VOICE Hello. This is the place, this is the only place for me. This is my mind. Welcome.

Blackout. Light up on JOE.

SCENE 1

JOE Scene One begins I'm asleep in my apartment on St. Mark's

Place, New York City, right above where it's *at*, right near where I work—the Underground Uplift, you know, head shop. We sell heads, other people's, mine especially. They come in off the street, dig it, they come in off the street, which belongs to the people. Which people? *The people.* One more *dig it*, one more *right on*, one more *rip off*, or bouncing teenage ass or pimply pout or ten-dollar Mick Jagger haircut, mister can you spare ten cents?, I need a fix—I'm asleep trying not to dream of leather wrist bands and freedom buttons—the freedom of the people is my iron maiden—and clever hash pipes—I'm asleep recovering from the daily revolution on St. Mark's Place, waiting for one of the early rehearsals of this play to begin. We're rehearsing in my apartment tonight. A peace and gladness play in which we teach the people how to bake bread. I dream of bread. I dream of dough. I'm asleep. I'm not quite conscious of the sounds of St. Mark's Place five floors below.

Light on JULIA. SHE *picks up the heavy shopping bag.* SHE's *walking down St. Mark's Place to* JOE's *house.*

JULIA   Scene One begins I'm walking down St. Mark's Place to Joe's apartment, carrying a shopping bag full of baking materials that our director asked me to bring over for him. He's going to be late. I don't understand the play, but it's work.

JOE, *as street person, hustles her for change. Brief improv.*

What's that? . . . No, I'm broke. . . . I said I was broke. He's cute. Julia, stop that. Is it wrong to like to . . . ? Julia, stop it. Is that Eric? *(Waves to a friend across the street)* Hi, Eric! . . . Guess it isn't.

SHE *has passed* MICHAEL. HE *hustles her for change. Brief improv.*

I don't have any change. . . . Michael's cute. I wonder if he's gay. Who's that? Oh, yes, the gorgeous bartender at Phebe's. I wonder if he's gay. Are all men gay? Some men are gay, some men aren't. Oh, Julia, you're so clever. Maybe Michael and I can go for a drink later at Phebe's. Julia, stop it. What time is it? Yes, I have time for a Coke. *(SHE's at a sidewalk stand)* A coke, please. . . . A coke. . . . *(More and more angry)* A coke, please. . . . Coke. Coke. . . . A *Coca-Cola!*

Light on MICHAEL. HE*'s still on the floor, pretending* HE*'s driving a car.*

MICHAEL Scene One begins I'm in my brand new mescaline purple Dart driving down to rehearsal from New Haven. The road appears to be straight but this is deceptive. *(As if* HE *were reading)* The road appeared to be straight but this was deceptive. Sun setting over People's Savings Bank, Bridgeport. Windshield wipers are stuck in the middle of the window. *(HE tries to fix them with one hand)* Wait a minute. Which people? Am I a people? No, I am a . . . flame. How do you tell people about — what do you even *call* it? Reality? God? How do you tell other flames that they *are* flames. . . . *(Tries to fix wipers again)* The wiring must have shorted. Julia, did you know that time is infinite? Watch that curve. Joe, time is infinite, bet you didn't know that. That means that— Wow, if time is infinite then— Asgrow Shrubbery Company . . . *(Has turned his head for a second)* Joe, on the way down tonight I held it together with Asgrow Shrubbery Company. Julia, I almost became a messiah on the way down tonight thinking about infinite time. Slow down—toll booth. *(Applies the brakes)* Julia, if it weren't for the toll booth and Asgrow Shrubbery I'd be in heaven right now. *(HE throws a quarter)* Look, kid, you *don't* want to be a saint —it'll cost ya a quarter.

JULIA *(Now in* JOE*'s apartment)* Middle of Scene One finds us in Joe's kitchen. *(To* JOE*)* ____ *(Director's first name)* said he was going to be late and in the meantime we should start without him.

JOE Then I said: *(To* JULIA*)* Start what?

MICHAEL *(Has quickly risen. "Drives his car" into* JOE*'s apartment.*

Makes the sound of brakes too quickly applied) Then I said in English: The improvisations, I suppose.

JOE In English as opposed to what?

MICHAEL Michael language.

JOE What are you on?

MICHAEL Myself.

JULIA Middle of Scene One finds us in Joe's kitchen. Michael and Joe are improvising an argument they never actually had but if they knew each other better they would have.

JOE *and* MICHAEL *ignore* JULIA.

JOE Kingdom of Heaven is within you?

MICHAEL Dig it.

JULIA I find myself laying out the ingredients for the bread we're supposed to bake in our director's absence. We've never done this before. *(SHE quickly empties the shopping bag onto the table)*

JOE Inside is outside?

MICHAEL Yes.

JOE Infinite time?

MICHAEL Yes.

JULIA What are you two talking about?

JOE Evil

MICHAEL   and goodness. Wholeness and

JOE   schizophrenia.

JULIA   Here are our aprons. *(Takes the red one for herself)* He said the red one was for me. Red as in lust.

JOE   *(Puts on the black one)* Black is for rage. Guess you get white, Michael. *(Throws the white one in* MICHAEL*'s face)*

MICHAEL   *(Sincerely)* I'm not pure enough for white.

JULIA   Michael, you say the oddest things. What's pure?

MICHAEL   Not wanting.

JULIA   We all *want* something.

MICHAEL   Is that good? Should we want?

JULIA   Are you serious?

MICHAEL   I'm sorry. You're right. I want not to want.

JULIA   I never know if you're serious.

JOE   He's serious. Look at him. *(To* MICHAEL*)* Tripping out on goodness, hmmm?

MICHAEL   Reality.

JOE   A reality trip maybe, reality no.

MICHAEL   My thing.

JULIA   *(Has been reading recipe. Quickly measures three cups of flour and puts them into medium-sized bowl. To audience)* End of Scene One: 3 cups of whole wheat flour.

MICHAEL   My thing.

JOE   You gonna show me your thing?

MICHAEL   You wanna see my thing?

JOE   If I can't see it it's not real.

MICHAEL   You really want to see my thing?

JOE   Yeah, I want to see it.

MICHAEL   If I show you mine will you show me yours?

JOE   Yeah.

MICHAEL   Ask me again.

JOE   Show me your thing.

This happens quickly, deliberately. MICHAEL *goes to bowl of flour. Takes a handful. Blows it into* JOE*'s face. Pauses.*

Is that your thing?

Blackout.

SCENE 2

Lights up quickly. A little time has passed.

JOE   I have something for eggs.

Tries to belt the cap pistol around MICHAEL*'s waist.* MICHAEL *keeps pulling it off.*

MICHAEL   Is this going to be a painful scene?

JOE   What do you mean painful?

MICHAEL   Do I have to hit someone or hate someone or make believe something unpleasant?

JOE   Look, flower children went out with "maryjane."

MICHAEL   And masochism went out with Masoch.

JOE   Put your crucifix where your mouth is. *(Goes into a Jesus-on-the-cross pose)*

MICHAEL   *(Sincere)* Om.

JOE   Om shit.

MICHAEL   *(Quietly)* There's enough hate and violence in the world.

JOE   I'm not a fucking saint.

MICHAEL   You drink too much! It fucks you up—makes you angry!

JOE   It's an angry ugly stupid world.

MICHAEL   Cool it; we're setting a bad example. *(Indicates audience)*

JOE   That's what they came here for: angry confrontation! *(Brings it to audience)*

MICHAEL   Om.

JOE   Talk about fucked up. He comes to rehearsal stoned out of his mind with a dumb grin on his face. Look, I went through that head shit in '66. The whole bit. Grass, acid, incense, Eastern religion—look, Buddha said the world is *pain*. Pain. *Pain*. PAIN. PAIN! Starving children, Kent State, Viet Nam. Augusta. Auschwitz. *Pain!!*

MICHAEL   Om.

JOE   Massacres at Mylai. *(*JOE *punctuates his statements with shots from the cap pistol)*

MICHAEL   *(Head bowed)* Om.

JOE   Blacks being shot at.

MICHAEL   Om.

JOE   John Kennedy.

MICHAEL   Om.

JOE   Martin Luther King.

MICHAEL   Om.

JULIA   *(Ignoring the argument. To audience)* The author says hello.

JOE   The Chicago Seven.

MICHAEL   Om.

JULIA   He was sitting at his desk—

JOE   The Berrigans.

MICHAEL   Om.

JULIA   His cat was sitting on his lap—

JOE   The Portland Eight.

MICHAEL   Om.

JULIA   He was upset—

JOE Pollution.

MICHAEL Om.

JULIA He thought of his friends—

JOE Preventive detention.

MICHAEL Om.

JULIA Manny and Lucy—

JOE Nixon!

MICHAEL Om.

JULIA And his mind cleared!

JOE *(Long pause. Calmer)* Come on, Michael. There're some nice parts to it. It's not *all* painful.

MICHAEL Get thee behind me, Satan.

JOE It'll help work out your aggressions.

JULIA *(Lifts* MICHAEL*'s arm. It falls back limp)* He's not aggressive.

JOE Help strengthen your ego?

JULIA He wants to weaken his ego.

JOE It'll help me work out *my* aggressions and help strengthen *my* ego. . . . *(No response)* I'll help you play God later? *(No response)* I'll sit there and go "Omkaram Bindhu Samyuktam." *(Yogic chant. No response)* I'll do my Mae West imitation? *(Falls into a Mae West pose. No response)* I'll do my soft-shoe number? *(No response)*

JULIA   Do your soft-shoe number.

JOE   Later.

MICHAEL   *(Has an idea. Playing stern)* I'll do your scene on one condition.

JOE   What's that?

MICHAEL   *(Still stern)* On condition that *(Sweet)* that you let me kiss you . . . full on the mouth . . . and in *full* view of the audience.

JULIA   *(Pissed)* Oh, Michael. That's childish.

MICHAEL   I am a child, a flower child.

JULIA   You're twenty.

MICHAEL   I'm nineteen.

JOE   I thought you were God.

MICHAEL   My condition.

JULIA   Michael.

JOE   Let the boy work out the scene the way he will.

MICHAEL   My condition.

JOE   All right. Where do you want me to stand?

MICHAEL *places him in position on his knees, his cheek to the audience.*

What is my expression?

MICHAEL *manipulates his face.* JOE *is wooden.*

Kiss me!

MICHAEL   *(To light booth)* Baby spot on Joe's face.

LIGHT MAN   What?

MICHAEL   *Baby on Joe's face!*

Lights dim. Baby spot on JOE*'s face.*

Julia, a drum roll.

JULIA   I don't have a drum.

MICHAEL   Rap on the table.

SHE *does a drum roll with spoons, aided by* MUSICIANS. MICHAEL *goes to* JOE. *Following done with full cognizance of the presence of the audience. A big production number.*

Close your eyes.

JOE *does so.*

Get ready. *(*MICHAEL *licks his chops obscenely)* Here goes! *(Just the lightest of pecks on the cheek)*

JOE   *(Still in position. Disappointed)* That it?

JULIA   *(To* MICHAEL*)* You're sweet.

MICHAEL   *(To* LIGHT MAN*)* Lights!

Lights, including the house lights, come up sloppily.

JOE   *(Gets up. To* LIGHT MAN*)* Get out the tape of war sounds. I'll need it in a minute.

LIGHT MAN   Which tape?

JOE   War sounds!

LIGHT MAN   I can't find it.

JOE   The author says: Where do they go from here?

LIGHT MAN   He's out of his mind!

JULIA   Our author is out of his mind.

JOE   The house lights are still on.

LIGHT MAN   What?

JOE   *(Yelling)* The house lights are still on!

LIGHT MAN   Sorry.

   House lights go off.

MICHAEL   *(To* JOE*)* What's your scene about?

JOE   Eggs.

MICHAEL   Dig it.

JULIA   Dig what?

MICHAEL   *(To* JULIA*)* You've been awfully silent.

JULIA   You're both crazy. He's drunk and you're high.

LIGHT MAN   *Dig it!*

JULIA   I just stand here mediating between a lush and a saint, saying lines I usually don't understand. Like now I say: *(To audience)* Hello out there. This is the author speaking. My mind grows cloudy.

MICHAEL   Om.

JULIA   *(Picks up egg)* If you say that once more I'll throw an egg at you.

JOE   Let's do my scene.

MICHAEL   *(Sarcastic)* I can hardly wait.

JOE *does a take.*

I didn't say that.

JOE   *(To* LIGHT MAN*)* Have you found the tape?

MICHAEL   I'm sorry, Joe.

LIGHT MAN   What?

JOE   Have you found the fucking tape?

MICHAEL   I'm sorry; I really am.

JOE   If you say that one more time!

LIGHT MAN   I'm looking.

MICHAEL   Om.

JULIA   *(Picks up egg again) Michael, shut up!*

LIGHT MAN   *Throw the egg!*

MICHAEL   Yeah, throw the egg!

> JOE *takes the egg from* JULIA *just in time.* HE *cracks it into the small bowl.*

JOE   Ovoid egg. Pretty yellow yolk. Protein-rich white. Albumin. *(Cracks another into bowl)*

MICHAEL   Seed of the universe.

JOE   *(Beating eggs with a fork)* Scrambled eggs.

MICHAEL   Unborn cousin.

JOE   Aborted chicken.

MICHAEL   Divine metaphor. . . . You're a sad man.

JOE   You're full of shit. *(Suddenly an idea)* Wait. That's it; I'm a sad man. I'm sad. That's the scene. *(To* LIGHT MAN*)* Skip the tape. *(To himself)* We are seeds of God when we are born but— *(To* MICHAEL *and* JULIA*)* Can you do a rap number?

JULIA   What do you mean?

JOE   Make believe you two are standing at a bar somewhere. You've just met. You're trying to pick each other up.

JULIA   Trying to pick each other up.

MICHAEL   *(Unsure* HE *can do this)* Joe—

JOE   You're at a bar somewhere—Max's, Phebe's, whatever.

JULIA   Someplace downtown.

MICHAEL   Who do I play?

JOE   Anyone.

JULIA   Anyone?

JOE   Anyone. One important thing: just keep rapping away no matter what I do—no matter what I do. *(To audience)* Scene whatever: 2 eggs beaten. *(To* MUSICIANS*)* Something blue. Something funky. *(To* LIGHT MAN*)* Bar lights!

Lights dim. Lighting suggests light from a juke box.

I'm a sad man. . . .

From this point to the end of the scene MICHAEL *and* JULIA *make
believe* THEY *are at a bar trying to pick each other up. The table
is a bar. At first* MICHAEL *can't get the hang of the situation, and*
JULIA *is too aggressive since* MICHAEL *is not saying anything.* JOE
will have to start his monologue over twice until HE *has coached
the two properly.* JOE*'s speech is performed on top of their
conversation. The music is, as* JOE *says, "funky."* THEY *might
sing:*

MUSICIANS

When the big man
Puts his shoe down
And opens up his vest,
You know that ain't no spansule, baby.

When Charlie Man-Tan
And Peggy Crosstown
Spiffy up their nest
With made-in-Asia
Psychedelic pissy plastic clapware,
You know that ain't no spansule, baby.

When Peter Potter
And Sondra Kaplan
Do their paper-daisy-op-pop-groovy, momma,
   Help, I'm dying—
   Lady, we're all dying—
Thing,
You know that ain't no spansule, baby.

When LeRoi LeRoi
And Ahmed Ahmed
Sock it to them,
Four hundred billion billion
Black blacks
With gun guns
In fifty million
Spade states,
Why they all sing—
Listen to them sing—
And all you freaks join in—
Let's sing—
That ain't no spansule, baby!

Some topics for MICHAEL *and* JULIA *'s rap: women's lib, encounter therapy, Zen cooking, drugs, orgies, communal living, water beds, ecology, rock music, etc. Their conversation will, of course, vary considerably from performance to performance. Some usable punch lines follow—*JULIA *has been acting too aggressive because of* MICHAEL *'s inactivity:*

[JOE   Julia, you're too aggressive.

JULIA   You said I'm trying to be picked up.

JOE   You're there trying to be picked up, but not necessarily for a fee.]

MICHAEL *has been unable to do the scene because he's been acting like* MICHAEL*; that is, sincere:*

[MICHAEL   Well, tell me how I should play it.

JOE   More plastic.

MICHAEL   How do you play plastic?

JOE   Forget it. Be yourself.]

JOE *gets drunker and drunker. There can be an imaginary bartender.* JOE *occasionally eavesdrops on the inane conversation of the other two.*

JOE   I was sad. Boy, was I sad. Man, I was sad. You wouldn't believe how sad I was. I sure was sad. Sad as a bitch. I mean I was sad. Sad, baby. You don't know what sad is. Sad as a nigger in a snowstorm. Sad as a honky with a tootsie roll. Sad as a woman scorned. Sad as a man with a *thing* and no one wants it and he's old and he's American and his wife just died and his kids are grown, and he's sitting in a steamroom working off a hangover with his gut hanging down to his balls, with his varicose veins staring him in the face, surrounded by faggots. *(Glances at* MICHAEL. *To* JULIA*)* You know, lady, you got a billion-dollar cunt. You know that? You got a fortune in pussy . . . Fill her up. Double. . . . I was so sad I'd have jumped off a roof, jumped under a train, leapt from a cliff, thrown myself into a fire, poured gasoline all over myself and thrown myself into those burning flames and gladly have died in pain. I'd have drowned myself in a public swimming pool surrounded by laughing children—No ice, this time. Straight. . . . I'd have drowned myself in the sea —I'd just lie there not swimming when I was supposed to, maybe near a shark or a poison jellyfish, lie there self-destructing, unreal, and let the water choke me. I was so sad and drunk in the gutter down and out—in the gutter down and out, in a doorway, out on the street with my head on the curb—no; in a doorway—drunk and not caring about the vomit—you know *(Proudly)*, piss in my pants, missed the fucking wall, *cocksucker!* Yeah, I know all about it and I don't give a shit, you hear me, motherfucker, I don't give a shit, take it and shove it, it's more than you've ever seen, or done, or ever hope *to do. (A fight)* Now look, I've taken all the crap I'm going to take— Oh, yeah— Oh, yeah— Oh, yeah— Oh, yeah— *(To* MICHAEL, *soberly, imperious)* Now push me to the floor.

MICHAEL   What?

JOE   Push me to the floor!

MICHAEL *does so, brutally.*

Now exit singing *"Age of Aquarius."*

Singing sourly, MICHAEL *and* JULIA *go stage left where* THEY *quietly sit with each other. Woodstock.*

Well, I don't give a *shit. Shit. Shit. Shit. Shit. Shit. Shit. Shit.* Don't shit me. *Shit. (Turns into a soft-shoe. "Shit" turns into the sound of a metal brush on a snare drum.* JOE *is Fred Astaire or Gene Kelly. Then a tap dance, drunken at first, then competent, magnificent. After tap number,* JOE *goes to his knees like Al Jolson)* I'm sad. I'm a sad man. It's all so fucking sad. Tell it to the wall! Tell it to City Hall! Tell the Pope! Tell God! *(Breaks mood. With fondness, to audience)* This is my favorite part.

Will begin to build. Each "sad" from here on is quickly echoed by MICHAEL *and* JULIA. *By the end the tempo is out-of-breath quick.*

Crying out to the universe and all the stars and the moons and planets, fuck it, I'm sad! Fuck it, stars! Fuck it, moon! Fuck it, I'm sad. Lying in bed I was sad. Sitting up I was sad. Climbing the stairs I was sad. Making love I was sad. My eyes were sad; my hands were sad. The floor was sad. The sky was sad and the flowers were drooping and sad with the rain and the rain was sad and the clouds were sad. A sad rainbow appeared and sadly the dim sun sank into the horizon of the sad city and the moon and sad Venus appeared and the street lamps shone sadly in the fog and I heard fog horns and police sirens and fire engines racing around crazy, sad. And sadly I went to sleep in a doorway—no—in the fire—no—in the sea. In a doorway. In the fire. In the sea. In a doorway, in the fire, in the sea, in a doorway in the fire in the sea in a doorway in the fire in the sea *(A broken record)* in a doorway in the fire in the sea in a doorway in the fire in the sea in a doorway in the fire in the sea in a doorway in the fire in the sea in a doorway in the fire in the sea in a doorway in the fire in the sea *(Repeat until phrase entrances actor—ten times or a hundred. As phrase regains meaning, words become erratic until, quietly)* in my bed.

MICHAEL and JULIA   *Sad!!!!!*

Blackout.

SCENE 3

Lights up. Some time has passed.

MICHAEL   *(Reading from recipe)* Let's see. "3 cups whole wheat flour, 2 eggs, ½ jar honey"—I have something for honey. Yes. *(To audience)* Scene Three: ½ jar honey. *(Picks up a copy of* The Upanishads*)* A little Eastern candy.

JOE   Michael, are you aware that you're a religious fanatic?

JULIA   *(To JOE)* It's all a game to him. Last week acid, this week Hinduism. Last month Buckminster Fuller, next month Laing.

MICHAEL   I suppose it looks that way. Let me read just a little. *(Finds his place in the book)*

JOE   *(To audience)* A word from the author:

MUSICIAN   *(Steps forward, sings solo directly to audience.* CAST *freezes in position)*

I'm just a man standing here before you,
Two feet on the ground,
Head in the stars,
And between them
The world of
Appetites,
The lovely mortal world of appetites.

They say the whole universe is spiral
From sea shells
To galaxies—
And reality
They say reality is also spiral.

They say what's inside is also on the outside.
Hells and demons
And incredible joy.
Joy and sadness
And madness.
Dimensions pass,
You find gladness.

I'm just a man standing here before you,
Two feet on the ground,
Head in the stars,
And between them
The world of appetites
The lovely mortal world of appetites.

CAST *"unfreezes" as if nothing had happened and continues
scene.*

MICHAEL *(To* JULIA. *Puts his arm around her. Tender)* You're a
funny little coo-coo.

JULIA Please stop talking baby talk.

MICHAEL *(Grabbing her breasts)* Gotcha boobies.

JULIA   *(Angry)* I'm not a toy.

JOE   He talks to me as if I were a child—

MICHAEL   I talk to you as if you were a Martian, only sometimes I'm not sure who's the Martian. *(Changes to mood of ecstasy)* I sure would love to read and stop this schizophrenia. That sure would make me happy. *(Looks at the two with a wonderful smile. Takes his book stage right and sits down to read it. A flagrantly "psychedelic" light shines on him. Reading aloud)* "This earth is honey for all beings, and all beings are honey for this earth. The intelligent, immortal being, the soul of this earth, and the intelligent, immortal being, the soul of the individual being—each is honey to the other. Brahman is the soul in each; he indeed is the Self in all. He is all.
"This water is honey for all beings, and all beings are honey for this water. The intelligent, immortal being, the soul of this water, and the intelligent, immortal being, the soul in the individual being—each is honey to the other. Brahman is the soul in each; he indeed is the Self in all. He is all.
"This fire is—

JULIA   *(She is now* MICHAEL*'s girlfriend)* Honey—

MICHAEL   "for all beings, and all beings are—

JULIA   Honey—

MICHAEL   "for this fire. The intelligent, immortal being, the soul of this fire, and the intelligent, immortal being, the soul in the individual being—each is—

JULIA   Honey—

MICHAEL   "to the other. Brahman is the soul in each; he indeed is the Self in all. He is all."

JULIA   *(To* MICHAEL *as if he were sleeping)* Honey, wake up. Honey, wake up. It's beautiful out. Let's bike up to the fountain.

MICHAEL *(Wakes up. HE starts crossing the stage, keeping his legs straight out in front of him. HE is walking on his buttocks. His arms are also stretched straight out in front of him. HE responds to JULIA and JOE kindly, but HE is detached from all human contact)* That's very kind of you to ask me but I'm going to heaven.

JOE Honey, come back to bed. I want to make love to you.

MICHAEL No thanks; it's nice here on the green road.

JULIA Honey, wait a minute. I'll pack your Pan Am bag. Do you want your toothbrush?

MICHAEL No thanks, Julia, I don't want my toothbrush right this moment.

JOE Honey, don't you want me to kiss you and love you all over and put my arm around your shoulder and tell you everything is all right?

MICHAEL What an interesting thought, but I don't want reassurance now. I see a pot of gold.

JULIA Honey, what should I tell the draft board if you go to heaven?

MICHAEL Sorry, Julia, but I can't answer your question. I have lost interest in communicating.

JOE Honey, I hate to be a drag but it seems that I've grown attached to you. Please tell me that you love me and need me.

MICHAEL *(Into his goal, speaking Michael language)* Ohibwa makaloona.

JULIA Oh, honey, are your political convictions changing? I didn't mean it when I said I would help you blow up the Chase Manhattan Bank.

MICHAEL   Mum dawney li grande la balyo.

JULIA   *(Proudly)* He has an answer for everything.

JOE   *(To JULIA)* Do you think he'll be coming back? *(To MICHAEL)* Honey, do you think you'll come back?

MICHAEL   *(Singing the same note)* La, la, la, la, la, la . . .

JOE   I wish you'd tell me so I can decide whether to try and build a relationship with Julia. I like Julia too.

MICHAEL   *(The road gets harder)* Lak, lak, lak, lak, lak . . . *(Building into an outburst)*

JULIA   *(To JOE)* I wouldn't hold it against you that you tried to take Michael away from me.

JOE   I hope you don't hold it against me that I tried to take Michael away from you. It was you I always loved. Deep down.

JULIA   I'll love you if you won't ask me to make bombs. I'm just a little girl and I'd like to finish school.

JOE   I love your tits. I'm happy when you put your tits in my mouth.

JULIA   It makes me happy when I make you happy. Here's a tit.

Shoves her breasts in JOE*'s face.* HE *sucks happily.*

I want to get a master's in Spanish. You won't mind if I study while you suck my tit. *(Recites like a child)* Quiero, quieres, quiere, queremos, queréis, quieren. Quiera, quieras, queramos, queráis, quieren. Quise, quisiste, quiso, quisimos, quisisteis, quisieron . . .

MICHAEL   *(Overlapping)* Lak-SHA!!!

MICHAEL's *shout knocks* JULIA *and* JOE *to the floor.*

JULIA   One cup milk.

MICHAEL   *(His moment of total unity with the All has degenerated into an argument with himself about primal unity versus conceptual duality.* HE *has reached his goal.* HE *is now stage left. Let one arm represent unity in this internal fight and the other duality)* A-voom, a-do, a-voom, a-do, a-voom, a-do, a-voom, a-do . . .

The argument peters out. JULIA *has gone to the table.* SHE *measures a cup of milk into a glass.* SHE *opens the can of nuts, which* SHE *then proceeds to chop up. Her chopping is heard under the rest of the scene.* JOE *helps* MICHAEL *to his feet. It is a struggle. What follows is in the style of* Zap Comix.

JOE   Mr. Monk, how are you?

MICHAEL   Monkly. How are you, Mr. World?

JOE   Worldly. How's the Holy Spirit treatin' ya?

MICHAEL   All right, I guess. Almost got there this time.

JOE   What stopped you?

MICHAEL   The usual. You know, fear of death.

JOE   Well, that's life.

MICHAEL   That's enough talk about me. *(Face to face, nose to nose, with* JOE*)* Gettin' any, hmmm?

JOE   Got me a new color television, a new job, joined the latest minority group. Oh, I married Julia.

JOE *waves to her at the table.* SHE *waves back.*

Oh—I almost forgot—you remember my pimple?

MICHAEL What pimple? The one behind your ear that was giving you trouble?

JOE No, the big one on my shoulder.

MICHAEL Isn't that a joke?

JOE *(Furious, almost insane)* Joke? Joke? Joke? *(Abrupt mood change back to light-hearted pleasantry)* Oh, yes, I see: a clash of dimensions. My head is a big pimple on my shoulders. I would find that funny if I could feel joy. Do you all like jokes here in your monastery?

MICHAEL Oh, yes.

JOE I'm disappointed.

MICHAEL Why?

JOE I thought you were beyond all that.

MICHAEL Beyond all what?—Oh, you mean *things of the flesh.*

JOE Yes.

MICHAEL Oh, no, very few of us are that advanced. We also suffer from a local meteorological problem.

JOE What's that?

MICHAEL Flesh storms. *(Advancing on* JOE, *who backs off)* Sometimes in the middle of the night, flesh—arms, legs, tits, asses, cocks *(*HE *rips off his shirt. Rubs his body all over* JOE*'s)*—appear from nowhere and they fly about. And just as suddenly as the storm began, it ends *(Stops trying to seduce* JOE*)* and the flesh disappears.

JOE That's terrible. And here I thought you'd be all happy, praying and cooking rice, prayin' and cookin' that ol' rice.

MICHAEL *attacks again.* JOE *tries to avoid the issue.*

Sniffin' the fresh air, weavin', choppin' wood, cookin' rice—
What's that smell?

MICHAEL Flesh storm! Take cover; they always begin this way. *(HE drags* JOE *to the floor)*

JULIA *(A crescendo of chopping)* One cup chopped nuts.

Blackout.

MUSICIANS *(An interlude, with light on them only)*

There ain't no way to heaven
And there ain't no way to hell
And there ain't no way to the sunny swimming pool,
'Cause there's a mighty blackness instead
And a lotta little holes
In the cloth that keeps us warm
In the cloth that keeps us dry
In the cloth that keeps out
Starlight, madness
    and
The clawing tiny fingers of rude and starving children,
The staring eyes of ladies and revolutionaries,
Promenading gaily in the ruins of the cities,
Dancing country dances on jettisoned French tables,
Shooting at the quarry of opposing losing factions,
Celebrating nightly what they think is man's due.

There's a growing mighty bald spot
In an optimistic beard.
The childlike smile of pleasure
Has become a dirty leer.

The overthrow of power
In the citadel of wealth
Is now an old pressed flower
In the chronicle of death by suffocation
    and
Sitting on another man's head.

No!
There ain't no way to heaven
And there ain't no way to hell
And there ain't no way to the sunny swimming pool
In a courtyard
On a lane
Over a hill
With napkins
And kittens
And a barnyard
And a mailbox
And oilcloth
And a radio
And a band-aid
And bacon
And ketchup
And peanut butter
Forever
With
You.

Crossfade lights from MUSICIANS *to center stage.*

SCENE 4

The mood is tender, nostalgic. JOE *and* JULIA *are sitting on the floor center stage, back to back.* MICHAEL *is standing behind them. To audience.*

MICHAEL   Scene Four: 1/2 teaspoon salt. (HE *measures salt into measuring spoon. Takes his place on the floor between* JOE *and* JULIA. *Let's say* HE*'s a tree* THEY*'re leaning against)*

JOE   You're driving in your brother's car, an old Volkswagen.

JULIA   With a sun roof that doesn't work.

JOE   Along a country road.

JULIA   In Connecticut.

JOE   In New York.

JULIA   In New York.

JOE   It's summer.

JULIA   Where'm I going?

JOE   Where're you going?

JULIA   I'm going to meet a man, another man, not you.

JOE   You're driving a pleasant sixty along an empty road to visit an old lover who'll make love to you in an old way. He's bought a bottle of fine wine for the occasion.

JULIA   I'm not sad and I'm not happy. I pass a car towing an old rowboat. A little girl in the back seat waves to me.

JOE   They're driving to a tiny house by the seashore. The house has a shower that needs to be fixed and a cracked mirror above the sink.

JULIA   Yes, the shower is made of white-enamelled metal; the floor is concrete. My lover pours wine into old jelly jars. One of them is cracked.

JOE   I haven't met you yet.

JULIA   You're still in San Francisco.

JOE   I'm studying mathematics and every Thursday night I play chamber music at a friend's house. We'll meet a year from now.

JULIA   Where will we meet? I know. At a rally—neither of us likes the speaker.

JOE   Or waiting in line for tickets to a rock concert we discover has been sold out.

JULIA   You're in San Francisco.

JOE   And you're riding along a country road in New York.

JULIA   Connecticut.

JOE   New York.

MICHAEL *starts singing the sad, lovely round* "Rose, Rose, Rose." HE *sings softly.* MUSICIANS *join in after a while.*

MICHAEL

> *Rose, rose, rose, rose,*
> *Tu ne seras jamais rouge.*
> *Oui, si je sais attendre,*
> *Mon bien-aimé.*

JULIA   I'm not sad and I'm not happy.

JOE   I'm not sad and I'm not happy.

JULIA   I'm not sad and I'm not happy.

JOE   I play chamber music every Thursday night.

JULIA   The car with the rowboat is headed toward the beach.

JOE   The shower has to be fixed.

JULIA   My lover pours wine into old jelly jars.

> JOE *and* JULIA *join* MICHAEL *in the round.* THEY *go to the table. There is no blackout.*

SCENE 5

> JOE *continues singing the round till his first line.* HE *might be doing jazz variations on the theme. His attitude toward the two younger people is that of detached amusement.*

JULIA   *(To audience)* Scene Five. Mix ½ cup oil and the honey. *(Pours oil into measuring cup. Empties measuring cup and the glass of honey simultaneously into the big bowl. To* MICHAEL*)* We meet.

MICHAEL   Add eggs. We fall in love. *(*HE *pours the small bowl of beaten eggs into the big bowl)*

JULIA   And then we get married. Milk?

MICHAEL   Then we go to Sweden. Milk. *(Pours the glass of milk into the big bowl)*

JULIA   Canada.

MICHAEL   Canada. Stir.

> JULIA *stirs the mixture in the big bowl.*

Wait. We stay.

JULIA   We stay?

MICHAEL   We ask the Tarot; we're indecisive. Stay or Canada?

JULIA   We get the Ace of Swords. You stir.

MICHAEL   *(Stirs)* We stay.

JULIA   I don't want to stay.

MICHAEL   *(An argument has been brewing)* And you didn't want to go. We ask the Tarot: guns or butter?

JULIA   Guns or butter. I don't like this.

JOE   *(Gently)* You ask the Tarot and you get the World Card. I'll mix. (HE *takes the bowl from* MICHAEL)

MICHAEL   The World?

JULIA   The World?

JOE   Which mixes you up and mixes you down, which mixes and mixes you. *(Checks recipe)* Mix together flour, salt, and nuts, and 4 teaspoons baking powder.

JULIA *helps him.*

Add to wet mixture. Stir. (HE *stirs)*

JULIA   Heavy.

MICHAEL   Heavy.

JOE   *(Referring to the dough)* It's getting lighter. A little more milk.

MICHAEL *pours in a little milk.*

JULIA   Wait! I had something to say about *milk.*

MICHAEL   I thought we got into milk.

JULIA   Yeah: butter and guns, guns and butter. Let's go back to: "And then we get married. Milk?" Okay? And then we get married. Milk?

MICHAEL   Then we go to Sweden. . . . Milk.

BOTH *of them get angry.*

JULIA   Canada. Milk.

MICHAEL   Canada. Stir. Wait. We stay.

JULIA   We stay?

MICHAEL   We ask the Tarot.

JULIA   Milk. We stay or we go.

MICHAEL   We ask the Tarot—

JULIA   Wait. We stay or we go—

MICHAEL   We ask the Tarot!

> JULIA *enters a trancelike state.* SHE *mixes the dough in a slow hypnotic rhythm during the first part of her speech. After a while* SHE *closes her eyes.* JOE *crudely mimes the actions and emotions mentioned by* JULIA. HE *might start off by playing a cameraman filming the action.*

JULIA   We stay or we go. We stay or we go. We stay or we go. . . . *(Pause)* In a small apartment . . . gasoline in the closet . . . the smell of caps? . . . firecrackers? . . . like a cap pistol . . . gunpowder?—gunpowder . . . a little child . . . not yours . . . a little naked kid with frizzy hair . . . he has a cap pistol . . . you have a gun . . . I give him milk in a baby bottle—a plastic squeeze bottle—I gave him milk from my breasts. *(Her eyes open wide; the look of a mind blown by an experience beyond one's conceptions; very brief moment, then her eyes close again)* Is he my child? . . . I gave him milk from my breasts— *(Mindblow)* Douglas, here's your milk— *(Mindblow)* Douglas, here's your milk— *(Mindblow)* Douglas, here's your milk—*(In pain)* It's time! Call St. Vincent's—pain— *(Mindblow)* Pain— *(Mindblow)* Pain—*(Abrupt change of mood to sexual ecstasy)* I love you I want your baby! *(Sexual pleasure)* I like it when you do that— *(Coy)* Don't come in here, I'm not dressed— *(Hollywood sexy)* I want you, wait— *(Cold rejection)* I don't want you— I want you, I don't want you, I want you, I don't want you. *(Takes the bit to the audience, choosing someone in the first row)* Want . . . want . . . want.

SHE *realizes where* SHE *is. Looks at the member of the audience* SHE *has chosen. Thanks him quietly. Goes back to the table. Looks at* JOE *and* MICHAEL *long and hard, but with new eyes.* JOE *might still be mimicking her gestures of "wanting" and "not wanting." Who are these furry creatures,* SHE *might be thinking.*

(To audience) Fill well-greased pans half full and let stand for 20 minutes.

SCENE 6

Some music, some lights to help the dough rise. A light show with live music if possible. Bright, quick, cheerful. Anything— rock, folk, gospel, a cheery Mozart chamber piece. The CAST *should clean up the mess they've made by now.* THEY *may talk to each other,* THEY *may dance. Scene Six should last from four to ten minutes, depending on the music.*

SCENE 7

MICHAEL *as a swami or guru.* HE *is no longer an insecure*

teenager. HE *speaks "as one having authority and not as the scribes."* JOE *and* JULIA *provide a background, chanting Yogic hymns such as Omkaram Bindhu Samyuktam—consult your local Yoga society for words and tunes. "***" is a holy word. It is to be pronounced "ah" or, better, let this sound be produced by finger cymbals.*

MICHAEL There is a this and there is a that. This is

JULIA *this and that.*

MICHAEL There is a here and there is a now. This is

JULIA *here and now.*

MICHAEL The

JULIA *that*

MICHAEL in the sun is

JULIA *thou.*

MICHAEL The

JULIA *this*

MICHAEL in the pointing finger is

JULIA *thou.*

MICHAEL The

JULIA *here*

MICHAEL is

JULIA   *everywhere.*

MICHAEL   The

JULIA   *now*

MICHAEL   is

JULIA   *eternity.*

MICHAEL   There is one and there is an other. There is you and there
is another. This is

JULIA   *you and another.*

MICHAEL   The

JULIA   *one*

MICHAEL   becomes the

JULIA   *other. You.*

MICHAEL   and

JULIA   *another*

MICHAEL   are sisters—

JULIA   *brothers.*

MICHAEL   This knowledge is beyond good and evil, pleasure and
pain. From this knowledge comes freedom. This knowledge is
the source of all that is. This is the fire, the center, the silence.
Whatever is tumbles forth from nothing eternally. This knowledge is ecstasy. This knowledge is ***.

Children of ***, go forth and know what you are. You are each of you, you are each of you, you are each of you the center of the circle. You are each of you, you are each of you, you are each of you the dancer of the dance. Which is your right foot, which is your left? The children are smiling, the lady is crying. Which is your right foot, which is your left? The babies are crying, the old man is dying. Which is your right foot, which is your left? The gas burns, the world turns. Which is your right foot, which is your left? Bear your birth-death; you are mother and father. Which is your right foot, which is your left?
Let the tears come. This is a time of tears. Then when we shall have cried, we shall each of us, we shall each of us, we shall each of us come to the center of the circle of ourselves again as it once is-was and hear—we all know the tune—yes, love, honey, dearest, brother, sister, ***, yes that's right, right, *right!* Lift up your right foot, lift up your left!

In the beginning that is always beginning
There was *** / There is *** / There will be ***.
One day *** knew that he was *** and became
-that-knows- and this knowledge was ***
Forever
Even now

ALL   *(Harmonizing)* Amen

Stage manager or director sneaks out bread during last part of MICHAEL's *speech. It is there for "Amen."*

SCENE 8

The CAST *offers bread to the audience.* MUSICIANS *play "Let Us Break Bread Together." Everyone eats.*

A QUICK NUT BREAD TO MAKE YOUR MOUTH WATER: Recipe from
Ehler's Whole Wheat Flour

½ jar honey
½ cup shortening
2 eggs—beaten
1 cup milk
½ teaspoon salt
4 teaspoons baking powder
1 cup chopped nuts
3 cups whole wheat flour

Mix shortening and honey, add eggs, then milk. Add dry ingredients mixed together and chopped nuts. Fill well-greased pans
half full and let stand 20 mins. Bake 1 hour in a moderate oven
of 350°. Makes 2 loaves 8″ × 4″ × 2½″.

SCHUBERT'S LAST SERENADE
Julie Bovasso

Schubert's Last Serenade is war—a lovely comic gem of a
war, illustrating the triumph of love over cold-hearted
society. Its own battle as a play opposes American romantic
spontaneity to the "alienation effect" of contemporary
European drama. The snobbery of headwaiters and the
Calvinist stubbornness of Thornton Wilder's grave Stage
Manager are combined in one rich image of repression
vanquished by the warmth of individuals.

CHARACTERS

THE MAITRE D.
ALFRED
BEBE
THE WAITER
THE COOK
FRANZ SCHUBERT

NOTE: The action of the play occurs exactly as described by the
MAITRE D. There are a few stage directions that are not spoken
by him; these are indicated in the usual manner. The MAITRE
D. stands outside the action of the play and should have no
contact with the actors, nor they with him.

The house lights fade to black. A single spotlight picks up the
MAITRE D. *standing at a lectern in a corner of the stage.* HE *reads*
from a manuscript.

MAITRE D.   An elegant French restaurant. In the darkness we hear
Schubert's Serenade played on a violin.

The music begins and the lights fade up very slowly on the scene.

Alfred, a young construction worker, dressed in overalls and hard
hat, is seated at a table with Bebe, a young Radcliffe sophomore
with a badly bandaged head. They stare at each other with
intense love. Behind a large potted palm Franz Schubert can be
seen through the leaves playing his violin. The waiter stands at
his station, napkin folded over his arm, waiting.

There is a long silence.

BEBE   I think it means something.

ALFRED   *(Nods)* Yeh.

BEBE   I mean . . . two people . . .

ALFRED   *(Nods)* Yeh, right.

MAITRE D.   The cook appears in the archway and shakes his fist fiercely at the palm tree. Franz Schubert stops playing and appears from behind the palm. The waiter looks from the cook to Franz Schubert. Franz Schubert looks from the waiter to the cook. The cook looks from Franz Schubert to the waiter; he makes another fierce gesture with his fist and exits angrily. The waiter follows him quickly off. Franz Schubert disappears behind the palm tree.

BEBE   I mean . . . it means something.

ALFRED   Yeh.

BEBE   Happenstance.

ALFRED   Yeh.

BEBE   Accident.

ALFRED   Yeh.

BEBE   Don't you think it means something?

ALFRED   Yeh.

MAITRE D.   Franz Schubert plays his serenade again.

There is a pause while the music plays.

Bebe brings her hand slowly up from her lap and moves it along the table toward Alfred. Alfred then brings his hand slowly up from his lap and moves it along the table toward Bebe. As their hands meet and touch they knock over a large glass vase.

The music stops abruptly.

The music stops abruptly. Alfred and Bebe rise in confusion and
embarrassment. Franz appears from behind the palm tree and
glares at them. The waiter appears with a dustpan and brush and
cleans up the mess. He glares at Alfred and Bebe and exits.
Franz Schubert disappears behind the palm tree, and Alfred and
Bebe resume their original positions and try to recapture their
love-spell. There is a long silence. Franz Schubert plays again,
and Alfred and Bebe recapture their love-spell. They sit staring
at each other with intense passion.

BEBE   Twice in two weeks.

ALFRED   Twice, right.

BEBE   It can't be an accident.

ALFRED   No.

BEBE   It has to mean something.

ALFRED   Right.

BEBE   It has to mean something.

ALFRED   Yeh.

MAITRE D.   The cook pokes his head through the archway again and
shakes his fist at the palm tree. The music stops abruptly. Suddenly, Bebe turns to the cook and shakes her fist fiercely at him.
He rushes off. Alfred wipes his brow nervously with the napkin.

ALFRED   Wow. Some goings on.

MAITRE D.   Franz Schubert plays again. There is another long pause
while Alfred and Bebe get back into their love-spell.

BEBE   I mean . . . why us?

MAITRE D.   Alfred nods. But he does not make eye contact.

BEBE   It's such a large city . . . millions of people . . . why us?

MAITRE D.   Pause.

BEBE   And twice. Twice in two weeks.

ALFRED   Right, twice.

BEBE   It's no accident.

ALFRED   No.

BEBE   It was planned.

ALFRED   Right.

BEBE   By some higher power.

ALFRED   Right.

BEBE   It was planned by some higher power that we should meet.

MAITRE D.   Bebe listens to the serenade, wistfully carried off by the romance of the moment. Alfred is uncomfortable and sits with his head down, glancing around with lowered eyes.

BEBE   I mean, you and me . . . from opposite ends of the stratum.

MAITRE D.   Alfred looks up, startled.

BEBE   Opposite ends of the stick.

ALFRED   Oh.

BEBE In a city with millions of people . . .

ALFRED Yeh.

BEBE We stumble . . . we fall. Twice.

ALFRED Right. We stumble . . . we fall.

BEBE Twice.

ALFRED Right.

MAITRE D. The waiter appears with two glasses of red wine. He places them on the table and, with a hostile glance at Alfred, exits. Alfred shifts uncomfortably in his seat. Bebe picks up her glass in a toast. Alfred does likewise.

BEBE You know . . . the first time we stumbled across each other, I fell.

ALFRED Oh, yeh?

BEBE Down there in front of the Customs Building. Did you fall for me the first time we stumbled across each other?

ALFRED Yeh.

BEBE I knew it.

ALFRED I didn't mean to crack your skull.

BEBE Oh, but it was meant to be. I mean . . . why *my* head? Why not some other head? Don't you see? Don't you understand?

ALFRED Yeh. I think so.

BEBE *Your* club found its way to *my* head. I mean . . . mine!

ALFRED   That's true. It was your head. Not some other head.

BEBE   Not just any head. Don't you think that's magical?

ALFRED   Yeh.

MAITRE D.   Franz Schubert stops playing and appears from behind
the palm tree. He stands looking at them with an expression of
unbelievable disgust.

BEBE   And just before I blacked out and fell, I knew that I had fallen.

ALFRED   For me.

BEBE   Yes. Just before I fell I knew that I was falling . . . for you.
Oh, I mean I was falling for The Cause . . . but while I was
falling for The Cause I simultaneously fell for you. It was a
double fall, you might say. The moment you raised your club I
started to fall. I fell even before you struck. But if you hadn't
struck, I wouldn't have fallen.

ALFRED   For me.

BEBE   No, for The Cause.

MAITRE D.   Franz Schubert scowls.

ALFRED   Would you have fallen for me if you hadn't fallen for The
Cause?

MAITRE D.   Bebe frowns suddenly and, with a nervous little gesture,
brings her hand to her chin.

BEBE   *(Evasively)* Have you got a cigarette?

ALFRED   *(Insistently)* Would you?!

BEBE   I really would like a cigarette.

MAITRE D. Alfred pounds his fist on the table.

ALFRED Answer my question!

BEBE What question?

MAITRE D. The cook and the waiter appear.

ALFRED If I hadn't cracked your skull with my club and given you cause to fall for your Cause would you have fallen for me anyway?

BEBE I don't understand the question.

MAITRE D. She starts to rise. Alfred grabs her roughly by the arm.

ALFRED Would you have fallen for me if you hadn't fallen for The Cause?

BEBE You're hurting my arm!

ALFRED Is it me or The Cause, baby?

BEBE You're making a scene.

ALFRED Let's have it straight or I'll break your skull!

MAITRE D. Bebe emits a cry of ecstasy and falls into his arms in a swoon. The waiter, the cook and Franz Schubert look from one to the other. Alfred holds Bebe's limp body, not knowing quite what to do with it. Finally he puts her back into her chair. The cook and the waiter exit with hostile glances at Alfred. Franz Schubert disappears behind the palm tree. Alfred sits stiffly in his chair. Bebe finally opens her eyes.

ALFRED Well?

BEBE I haven't been quite honest with you.

ALFRED   That's what I thought.

BEBE   If you hadn't struck me that first time and given me the opportunity to fall for The Cause I might not have fallen for you at all.

MAITRE D.   Alfred rises angrily . . .

ALFRED   That's what I thought!

MAITRE D.   . . . flings his napkin on the table, picks up his tool box and leaves.

BEBE   Alfred, wait! Don't leave like this. Give me a chance to explain. It's all very complex. Please don't destroy something precious. It was the second time that I was really hooked, and whether or not the first time had happened the second time would have happened anyway.

MAITRE D.   Franz Schubert has come out from behind the palm tree and stands listening with interest.

BEBE   Don't you see? Whether or not I knew consciously that first time whether I had fallen for you because you'd made me fall for The Cause or whether I'd have fallen for you anyway doesn't matter. It was the second time, on the Gansevoort Street pier.

MAITRE D.   Franz Schubert is confused.

BEBE   That second time was the time I knew that this time it was for real.

MAITRE D.   The waiter has entered with the cook.

BEBE   When I saw you marching on that line in front of the pier carrying that picket sign which read "Save the Pier," and I arrived carrying a sign which read exactly the same thing! Oh,

Alfred! That was the moment. It was the moment I realized that *we were on the same side!*

MAITRE D.   She pauses and waits for some reaction. None is forthcoming. Desperately, she turns to Franz Schubert, the cook and the waiter for help.

BEBE   Don't you see? I realized that we were on the same side!

MAITRE D.   They shrug.

BEBE   *(Turning back to* ALFRED*)* You, who had cracked my skull viciously two weeks earlier and sent me reeling to the ground for my cause!

MAITRE D.   Alfred does not respond. She turns to Franz Schubert, the cook and the waiter again and attempts feverishly to explain.

BEBE   *(To* FRANZ*)* Don't you see? All my mixed emotions suddenly came together. All the confusion of love and hate jelled.

MAITRE D.   Franz Schubert looks at the waiter.

BEBE   *(To the* WAITER*)* Love jelled into hate . . .

MAITRE D.   The waiter looks at the cook.

BEBE   *(To the* COOK*)* Hate jelled into love . . .

MAITRE D.   The cook looks at Franz Schubert.

BEBE   And suddenly I understood everything!

MAITRE D.   They all look at each other in total confusion.

BEBE   *I understood my feelings about that first time at the Customs House!*

MAITRE D. Bebe turns desperately to Alfred, who is still not listening.

BEBE I understood why I had felt that gnawing guilt about loving you, Alfred!

MAITRE D. At the mention of his name, Alfred turns.

BEBE And because of that guilt I had denied the truth to myself. I understood why I wanted to fling myself into your arms the moment you raised your club. I understood why I wanted to wrap myself around you and kiss you madly on the eyes in front of the world while the clubs were swinging and the rocks were flying and the bricks were hurtling through the air!

MAITRE D. The cook and the waiter leave. Franz Schubert straightens his tie selfconsciously and goes behind the palm tree.

ALFRED Are you saying that you would have fallen for me anyway? Even if I hadn't clubbed you?

BEBE Yes!

ALFRED Okay.

MAITRE D. They return to the table and resume their love spell with even greater intensity. Franz Schubert plays again . . . slightly off key.

The music plays for a while, slightly off key, before BEBE *speaks.*

BEBE You know, Alfred . . . life is funny.

ALFRED Yeh.

BEBE I might not have known it if the second time hadn't happened.

MAITRE D.   Alfred is immediately suspicious.

ALFRED   *(Suspiciously)* Waddayamean?

BEBE   I mean the Gansevoort Street pier. When I saw that we were on the same side it substantiated all the irrational emotions which I experienced at the Customs House.

ALFRED   Oh, right.

BEBE   You were fighting to save the pier. I was fighting to save the pier . . .

ALFRED   *(Pause)* It's the Union. The Union is behind it all. The Union is behind everything.

BEBE   The Union is behind its men.

ALFRED   The men are behind the Union.

MAITRE D.   Franz Schubert appears from behind the palm tree with a savage look on his face.

BEBE   The Union is behind our love.

MAITRE D.   Franz Schubert flings his violin violently across the room. Alfred and Bebe rise in confusion. Franz, in a state of utter agitation, is feverishly mopping his face with a handkerchief. He then crosses the room and picks up his violin. The waiter enters hurriedly and tries to calm Franz Schubert, patting his head and brushing off his coat. Then, with an angry glare at Alfred and Bebe, he takes Franz behind the palm tree. Alfred approaches them.

WAITER   *(Coldly)* Would you like to order now, please? The cook is getting impatient.

ALFRED   Oh, yeh. Sure. We'll order now. Fine.

BEBE No! We'll wait!

MAITRE D. The waiter glares at her with fury, turns abruptly and exits.

ALFRED You shouldn't have done that. He's really mad. Maybe he needs the table.

BEBE Posh. We're not here to accommodate him; he's here to accommodate us.

ALFRED That's true. I never thought of it that way.

MAITRE D. Franz Schubert comes out from behind the palm tree. He has completely recovered his composure and his manner is very disdainful and haughty. He moves to a table upstage and sits, crossing his legs and looking smugly at Alfred and Bebe. They glance at him; he smirks back at them and turns away with a derisive grin. He then raises his hand and summons the waiter.

ALFRED *(Leaning across the table and whispering)* He's mad, too. I don't think he's going to play anymore.

MAITRE D. The waiter enters with a glass of wine for Franz Schubert. Franz raises the glass in mock toast to Alfred and Bebe. The waiter laughs. Then Franz Schubert laughs with the waiter.

ALFRED I'll rap 'em both in the head.

BEBE Don't pay attention to them. They're trying to arouse us. If we ignore them they'll stop.

MAITRE D. Alfred glares angrily at Franz Schubert and the waiter, who smirk back at him. The waiter then leans over to Franz and whispers something in his ear. Franz nods. The waiter laughs. Then they both laugh and glance at Alfred and Bebe.

ALFRED I'll break that violin over his fat head!

MAITRE D. Alfred rises.

BEBE No, Alfred, no. Sit down. I hate violence.

ALFRED *(Advancing on* FRANZ SCHUBERT *and the* WAITER*)* Did you hear me? I'll break that violin over your fat head!

MAITRE D. Franz Schubert scurries behind the palm tree and the waiter rushes off into the kitchen. Alfred stands in the center of the room with his fists clenched and bellows loudly.

ALFRED *(Bellowing loudly)* Let's have a little service around this dump!

BEBE Alfred, please. You're making a scene. Sit down.

ALFRED What is this shit around here? Who the fuck runs this joint? What kind of help have you got in this freak-house restaurant?

BEBE Alfred, please. Come and sit down.

MAITRE D. Franz, the waiter and the cook have appeared.

BEBE We were talking about us, Alfred, remember? Us.

MAITRE D. Bebe tugs at his sleeve and finally gets him back to the table, but Alfred is still preoccupied with his anger.

BEBE Look at me, Alfred. Love. It's the only solution.

MAITRE D. Alfred rises suddenly and slams his fist on the table and shouts at the waiter, pointing his finger directly at him in a commanding manner.

ALFRED You! Bring us some menus!

MAITRE D. The waiter rushes off. Alfred turns to Franz Schubert.

ALFRED   You! Go play your violin!

MAITRE D.   Franz Schubert disappears behind the palm tree and plays frantically, at a much faster tempo. Alfred turns to the cook.

ALFRED   You! Get back into your kitchen, quick!

MAITRE D.   The cook hobbles off. Alfred sits. Bebe stares at him with admiration.

BEBE   You're marvelous.

ALFRED   *(Modestly)* It was nothing.

BEBE   No, it was something. It really was something. I mean . . .

ALFRED   It was nothing, nothing.

BEBE   . . . to be aroused to such passion, such fury, such . . .

ALFRED   It was nothing.

BEBE   Just like that! Without any cause.

MAITRE D.   Alfred is immediately on his guard.

ALFRED   Waddayamean?

BEBE   I mean . . . I envy you. I really do. I mean . . . I wish I could be aroused without any cause.

ALFRED   Waddayamean, without any cause? I had a cause. They caused it.

BEBE   Well . . . small cause to warrant such a big reaction.

ALFRED   Oh, yeh?

BEBE   You overreacted.

ALFRED   Oh, yeh?

BEBE   And I suspect it's because you don't have a larger cause to react to.

MAITRE D.   She leans over and touches his hands gently.

BEBE   Poor Alfred. If only you could harness your fury to an Ideal.

ALFRED   *(Pulling his hands away)* Getattaheah.

BEBE   What's the matter? You're suddenly angry with me.

ALFRED   Yeh, I'm angry. I'm angry as hell. First you say I'm marvelous and then you take it all back.

BEBE   I didn't take it all back. I simply adjusted my initial reaction.

ALFRED   You adjusted it all right.

MAITRE D.   He rises angrily . . .

ALFRED   You threw a wet rag on the whole thing.

MAITRE D.   . . . flings his napkin on the table . . .

ALFRED   Shit!

MAITRE D.   . . . and starts to leave.

ALFRED   I'm going home.

BEBE   No, Alfred, please. Don't leave like this. Why can't we discuss things without getting angry and walking out? You're so compulsive, so irrational. You don't leave any room for differences. If you don't like something you get up and walk out. That's running away, Alfred . . . running away from infinite possibilities.

ALFRED   Yeh? Well, I'm still going home.

BEBE   I want to understand you, Alfred. I want to know you. And I want you to understand me and know me. What good is love without understanding? How can we love each other if we don't know each other and understand each other? How can we understand each other if we don't know each other? And how can we know each other if we don't love each other . . .

ALFRED   Okay.

MAITRE D.   Alfred returns to the table, somewhat sullenly. There is a long silence. Bebe observes him clinically.

BEBE   *(Patronizingly)* Why did you come back?

ALFRED   What?

BEBE   Why did you come back?

ALFRED   *(Angrily)* I came back because I came back.

BEBE   *(Persisting)* But why? Why did you come back? Do you *know* why? Have you thought about it?

ALFRED   No, I haven't thought about it. I haven't had time to think about it.

BEBE   There you go getting angry again. Why are you angry? What did I say to make you angry? (SHE *begins to cry)* I can't open my mouth without you shouting at me. Every word I say, you shout at me . . . like a bully.

MAITRE D.   The cook enters disguised as a lady flower seller.

ALFRED   Do you want a flower? Don't cry. I'll buy you a flower. Hey, you!

The COOK *crosses to their table.*

Which one do you want?

BEBE   That one.

SHE *takes the flower and* ALFRED *gives the* COOK *a dollar.* BEBE *sits sniffing it for a moment.*

It doesn't smell. It's fake.

MAITRE D.   She flings the flower on the table. Alfred picks it up and sniffs it.

ALFRED   You're right. It's fake.

MAITRE D.   He rises quickly and begins to bellow again.

ALFRED   Fake! She sold us a fake flower! Where did she go? Hey! Flower seller! Come back here, you fake! We don't want your fake flowers, understand?

MAITRE D.   Franz Schubert and the waiter appear.

BEBE   Alfred, sit down. It doesn't matter.

ALFRED   Waddayamean, it doesn't matter? *(To* FRANZ *and the* WAITER*)* Where's that flower seller? She sold me a fake flower.

BEBE   Alfred, sit down, please. You're making a scene. It's nothing.

ALFRED   Waddayamean, it's nothing! It's a fake. And a fake is a fake. When I buy something real I don't want it to be fake.

BEBE   It doesn't mean that much. It's only a flower.

ALFRED   It's not a flower, it's a fake. A flower is a flower and a fake is a fake and I can't stand anything that's fake. Fake is shit! I shit on fake!

BEBE   This is embarrassing. Alfred, I don't care about the flower. It doesn't mean that much to me. Please, sit down.

MAITRE D.   Alfred finally calms down and sits. Franz Schubert disappears behind the palm tree; the waiter starts to leave but decides not to.

BEBE   You see what I mean? You get so violent and passionate over such small things.

ALFRED   It's not a small thing.

BEBE   It's only a flower.

ALFRED   It isn't a flower!

BEBE   It isn't the end of the world.

ALFRED   It's the idea behind it!

BEBE   There is no idea behind it. You feel cheated, that's all.

ALFRED   All! All! Damned right I feel cheated! And that's not all! I feel so fucking cheated over that goddamned fake paper flower . . .

MAITRE D.   He picks up the flower and rips it to shreds . . .

ALFRED   Fake . . . fuck . . . !

MAITRE D.   . . . and flings it into the air.

ALFRED   I hate anything that's fake!

MAITRE D.   Exhausted, he sits down, his head in his hands. Bebe strokes his back gently.

BEBE   I understand. Poor Alfred. You get so passionate over nothing.

ALFRED   That's why I clubbed you. Because you gimme that fake smile. Fake!

BEBE   *(Startled)* What?

ALFRED   Yeh, yeh, fake. Waddaya think, I'm blind? I seen the expression on your face when I raised my club down there at the Customs House. You were ready to kill. You were ready to tear me apart, and I thought, Wow! This chick is outa sight. This chick is gonna beat the living shit outa me! But no! Waddaya do? You cop out, that's what. Pppftt! Just like that. Sudden. You go soft on me and you smile. You gimme that little Jesus-Christ-on-the-cross smile, and in a second I know that you want me to club you. You expect me to club you. So I club you! Otherwise you wouldn'ta gimme that fake smile. You woulda tore into me the way you really wanted to. You'da scratched my face and bit my flesh and kicked me in the balls, and I'd of thought, Wow! This is a real chick! But no. Waddaya do? You stop. You stop just long enough to . . . adjust your initial reaction . . . and you fake out! Fake! Fake! Fake! Somebody should've split your skull long ago, let you know where it's at!

BEBE   You really are a beast, aren't you? An animal. And you're a coward on top of it all. Oh, big strong man with a steel hat and a club, coming at a lot of defenseless women and students . . .

ALFRED   Fakes. Fakes. And I hate anything that's fake. You're no woman. You're a fake. Fake-out. Fake.

BEBE   Oh, how could I have deluded myself into thinking I loved you? You are the lowest, the most primitive, the most despicable . . .

ALFRED   Right! But I'm real. I'm not fake!

BEBE   You're everything I've always loathed. How can I have imagined that I loved you?! How is it possible? How can I have even conceived the idea? Oh, Daddy. Daddy. All these years I've despised you, Daddy, because you were a gentleman, a man of refinement, a man of sensibilities, a man of education . . . Quiet, understanding, always willing to sit down and discuss a problem. Oh, Daddy, Daddy. I've betrayed you, Daddy. Betrayed you with this beast!

MAITRE D.   The waiter approaches the table.

WAITER   Excuse me, sir. I'll have to ask you to remove your hat.

ALFRED   Remove my hat?

WAITER   Yes. We don't permit gentlemen in the dining room with their hats on. A gentleman always removes his hat.

ALFRED   I'm sorry, but I'm not removing my hat.

WAITER   You'll have to leave unless you remove your hat.

ALFRED   I'm not removing my hat and I'm not leaving!

BEBE   (Screaming) Oh, God. Oh, God. You're making a scene. Take off the hat!

ALFRED   Shaddap!

BEBE   My father would take off his hat!

ALFRED   I'm not your father!

BEBE Oh, God!

WAITER Why won't you take off your hat?

ALFRED Because it's my hat!

WAITER *(To* BEBE*)* Why won't he take off his hat?

BEBE Because it's a symbol. Not a hat. If he takes it off he'll have an identity crisis.

WAITER I see. *(*HE *exits)* Bebe rises and begins to collect her things.

ALFRED What are you doing?

BEBE I'm leaving, that's what I'm doing.

ALFRED Leaving?

MAITRE D. Alfred rises and grabs her arm.

ALFRED Waddayamean, leaving?

BEBE It's over. Let go of my arm.

ALFRED Waddayamean, over? Where do you think you're going?

BEBE Home. It's all over. Finished. I don't love you. It was a mistake.

ALFRED Waddayamean, a mistake?

BEBE Let me go!

MAITRE D. Bebe pulls away and rushes toward the exit.

ALFRED What's a mistake? Come back here.

MAITRE D.   Alfred grabs her again. She struggles.

BEBE   Let me go. It was all an illusion. A mistake.

ALFRED   Well, which was it, an illusion or a mistake?

BEBE   Let me go, you brute!

MAITRE D.   Alfred cracks her across the jaw.

The actor does not follow this direction. The MAITRE D.

MAITRE D.   Alfred cracks her across the jaw.

The actor still does not follow the direction. HE *holds* BEBE*'s arms.*

ALFRED   You can't go. I dig you.

MAITRE D.   Bebe screams and rushes off.

The actress does not follow this direction. THEY *both remain fixed, looking at each other. The* MAITRE D. *repeats the direction very firmly.*

Alfred cracks her across the jaw. Bebe screams and rushes off.

BEBE   *(Softly)* You called me a fake.

ALFRED   So what? So you're a fake. I dig you.

MAITRE D.   *(Shouting) Alfred cracks her across the jaw. Bebe screams and rushes off.*

BEBE   You said you hate fakes.

ALFRED   I do. But I still dig you.

MAITRE D.   *(Commanding like a Nazi) Alfred cracks her across the jaw . . . !*

ALFRED   . . . and something is telling me that I oughta crack you across the jaw but I don't want to.

MAITRE D.   Bebe screams and rushes off.

ALFRED   Because I dig you.

MAITRE D.   *Bebe screams and rushes off!*

BEBE   *(Softly)* I dig you, too.

MAITRE D.   *Bebe screams and rushes off, do you hear what I am saying?!!*

BEBE   And something is telling me that I should leave, but I don't want to. It's as though something has always been telling me to do one thing when I've wanted to do something else. It's been that way all my life . . .

MAITRE D.   *(Desperately) Alfred cracks her . . . across the jaw . . .*

ALFRED *kisses* BEBE *tenderly.*

Bebe screams . . . and rushes . . . off . . .

WAITER   Franz Schubert appears from behind the palm tree, smiling.

FRANZ SCHUBERT *appears, smiling.*

MAITRE D.   *(Whirling on the* WAITER*)* You're fired!

FRANZ SCHUBERT   *(Raising his bow)* Franz Schubert raises his bow and begins to play, magnificently.

MAITRE D. You're all fired!

FRANZ *has begun to play, magnificently. The* COOK *appears with a tray of coconuts.*

COOK The cook appears with a tray of coconut milk.

MAITRE D. What coconut milk! I will have no coconut milk!

WAITER The Maitre D. flings his script across the room, kicks over the lectern and charges off like an angry savage.

MAITRE D. *(Flinging his script across the room, kicking over the lectern and charging off like an angry savage)* You're all fired! Through! Finished! Do you hear! You're finished, Schubert! D'ya hear me!? Finished! And you! And you! And you! And you!

WAITER The waiter hands a coconut to Alfred, to Bebe and to the cook, and they all drink their coconut milk while Franz Schubert plays, magnificently.

The music swells and the lights fade on ALL *drinking coconut milk.*

BA-RA-KA
Imamu Amiri Baraka
(LeRoi Jones)

Imamu Amiri Baraka dips his own being into a new
definition of genesis. His is at once the story of his own and
the black race's birth. Authentic knowledge of the self
changes us forever. We can never draw back, and the
blood-strength of his poem-play-ritual washes over our
"selves," destroying the useless and redundant parts of the
individual's existence. LeRoi Jones is reborn and, with the
stern power of the magician, names himself anew and is
Ba-Ra-Ka.

PREFACE *read to black silence with hint of light way off   is read w/ slow slight gradual in background a red sound develops until opening:*

"Before the universe was inhabited wisdom was invisible blood and thots congealed under postmanifestd pressures.

The degree of our sight
is the end of the night
the sun is our selves
the stars are others suns, other selves,
in the absolute darkness of the living being
the soul of creation
the sole being
the only
the lonely
smiling in the outer reaches past the final deaths of things
that cannot be
born"

"In the dark   ness
harmonized with it all
a big tune
swarms kissing mouths
    universes
        cells
            tunnels
                whoremartyrs' shapings

Athe body
athe flesh
athe vision
athe at up
    a the at up side down
        a the at up side side down
            this
            athis

athis
lying flat without shadow
it can cast its compass up full spread a holy woman man a heaven
been

athe, body
trapped inot works
love pulled
arch of trinity 3, and it is and kings
the kings ride, wide
this is their road
3,
3,
kings ride, flat square holds
its stretched love of
3's the point, the father
the son
and alotta laughing all over the
space"

BA-RA-KA

MEN *come out and fight. Brutally*
THEY *fight and fight. The lights go up and down.* THEY *fight and
scuffle*
*wallow on the floor, try to kill each other. (Slow lights then fast,
Light is Red. Direct.
Everything Red.)*

Black

MAN *comes out   moves forcefully. Cuts down. Sweeps across. Moves
everything.
Lifts everything. Throws everything. Is supremed.
Lights are Red. Then intense Red. Then out.*

MEN *come out scuffling*

MAN *comes out sweeping and moving forcefully.*
MAN *in corner illuminated with Yangumi moves.*
Red intensity. Screech of Red sound. (check).

MAN *comes out Yangumi-dance. Screech and red intense light.*
Now BLUE MAN *comes out. Is revealed. In blue, in intense blue light.*
HE *opens arms to take all to embrace all.* HE *is intent in his openness,*
to be so open, to everything. HE *is upstage of the* YANGUMI. YAN-
GUMI *stops and punches.*
Black out.
Only the BLUE
and blue   ness the openness, the wise sound of a blue know come
around and move him in a rhythm of understanding.

Now the BLUE *and* RED *are up and downstage, as the light goes off*
to reveal them switched, ONE *up the* OTHER *downstage. The intense*
red on the puncher, the tight jawed the. the blue on the open armed
the open faced. the.

Now a THIRD MAN, *in Green. Intense Green. Wavering from Red to*
Blue as the other lights pass over the green. These lights waver and
the THIRD MAN *wavers but as a chord of sound. A green sound*
bathes him and his movement. HE *is seen alone. And then at midpt*
soz that HE *makes a connection between the other two intensi-*
ties.
The RED *stalks to the one corner punching.*
The BLUE *floats to the other corner welcoming.*
The GREEN *darts from one to the other*

THEY *resolve as a circle.*
THEY *resolve as the three points with green centered*
THEY *resolve as a triangle, all other forms moving, the triangle fixes a*
pyramid.

WOMEN *come out dressed in brown.* THEY *lay upon the floor and the*
and rolatten.

Now a white light intense and moving through the entire spectrum
with the colored tints. plays on the WOMEN. *who are sprawled to*
form a square. THEY *open their legs to form the square.* THEY *roll*
back and forth on the floor as the light beats on them. As the tints
pass THEY *pass to different attitude, the baked, the wet, the giving*
the green THEY *hold up to show the growth up out of their fe-*
maleearth selves. As the SONS *run and sprawl on them, and make*
the symbolic covering, covering them as THEY *turn, and the spec-*
trum moves from color to color. And THEY *make the sounds of the*
earth. The roar of fire. From the RED MAN. *And the* SUN MEN. *The*
coool rain sounds of blue and blues chants from the SUN MEN *and*
the BLUE MAN *moans and their own child visioning moans of ecstasy.*

And the GREEN *stands up. Green in their hair. Around their out thrust*
arms as if they were gesturing at their lover the sun who goes away
each night tho they hold his heat and light and change the wetness
of their flesh.
Now RED *and* BLUE *at each side of the square lean in to the center*
holding the GREEN *who is three yet one.*
And HE *is speaking moaning singing*

SUN & SHADOW

"All that life is is in this act of self recall.
And We are lovers lovers alll. Embrace ourselves.
and God. The single eye is God and life and harmony.
This is the pyramid of our lives. Our thrust from
nothings to beings
We are life. We are each other
We are the whole. The holy beings.
Understand the infinite understand the divine
All beings are one but the shadow is not the sun

repeat (in african-blues-"jazz"-newblack-r&b thang)

All beings are one,
yes yes

all be
ings
are one one one
ye
es
all be
ings
are one, sweet people
but god knows
the shadow
is not
is not
no the shadow
cant be
la, simba,
the shadow
is sho not
the sun"

GREEN *reaches*
ALL *reach*
lay out flat like a huge sun and begin moving wiggling slowly clockwise
  around the floor, smaller circle standing counter clockwise inside,
  the one, inside.
slowly

  Black.

HE WANTS SHIH!
Rochelle Owens

For Paul Blackburn

We see the face of the howling monkey. China has been
for the West cheap labor, converts, trade, opium. China
was a carcass of worms. . . . China now deplores the
tradition of conspicuous consumption. In this play the
irrational happens: *China is so big.* The heart lies like the
vulnerable jelly it is. What is the Westernization of people?
Excessive largeness intimidates. *China is so big.* Where does
the little one go? The Western world is a scintillating face:
fact of—unnatural nature—human experience. What is the
burden of life? Anarchy "licks" on Tuesday and exalts on
Wednesday—astonishes—astonishes. Socialism strives for
the perfection of the world; art does too. I don't know the
Chinese language—in this play the irrational happens: I
know the Chinese language. You find China here—in your
own environment study acupuncture. In the West and in
the East the monks are holy capons, desexed chickens,
neuters. They walk "different." Feng/Fong. Fong is the
way it sounds, like dong. A bell. There is a tradition of
ghastly consumption. Fong is sensual. Love your own
visceral living moment of energy and you will whet
appetites. Forget all aspects of "naturalism": it died in the
year of the centipede. The word "shih" means everything.
It has other meanings also, depending on tonal sounds, but
everything shih is all I care about.

CHARACTERS

THE EMPRESS
DAGAROO, the eunuch
NEETO, a peasant
SUPTI, a peasant
MIM, a peasant
BOK, the stepbrother of Lan
LAN, the Emperor of China
PRINCESS LING
FENG, the monk who is Lan's mentor
KLINGER, an American
GRABHARDT, an American
LI HANG, a Buddhist
KANG, a Buddhist
OTHERS: Dancers, soldiers, monks, crowds

ACT I / SCENE 1

War in China. The last EMPRESS *of the Manchu dynasty is with her eunuch slave,* DAGAROO. *From outside low chanting is heard. Lights in brilliant colors are flashing. . . it is the mood of celebration and* change.

EMPRESS *(Smoking her opium pipe)* They are not playing the flute.
. . . *(Shakes her head slowly)* Listen . . . no flute . . . in old times
we listened to the flute. . . . Are you listening . . . Dagaroo?

The EUNUCH *smiles grotesquely.*

You are not . . . listening . . . Dagaroo . . . but China's raw wound
is in your face . . . that you can feel . . . you are not dead. *(Laughs)*
Let me see your blue tongue. . . .

HE *sticks out his tongue.*

Sickness starts in the low intestine . . . there is most likely too much black bile in you . . . it makes your tongue blue. *(SHE lies down)* Dagaroo . . . you play the flute.

HE gets the flute and plays. SHE falls asleep. DAGAROO watches her, then slowly goes to the door and calls out in a shrill high sound. THREE PEASANTS enter and go up to the sleeping EMPRESS and touch her body with their fingertips.

NEETO *(Intensely)* She is without a tail!

MIM *(Angrily to DAGAROO)* Who cut off her tail! Did you!

DAGAROO shakes his head, his face is masklike.

EMPRESS *(Speaking in her sleep. Her voice is rhythmical)* Cover the animal sheng tai kei hold down her toes fingers one hundred one thousand driven down man kuo monkeys jaws teeth thick fat bodies shrunk female male spread this and that way black rottings, China wraps up the heads of the newly born. . . . Ends and completes us.

NEETO The yellow Buddha says to use a carving knife! I do not own a carving knife! *(HE removes from his cloak a red hatchet and chops off a hand of the EMPRESS. SHE groans in her sleep. HE laughs)* She is without a hand! *(HE touches the edge of the hatchet)* The blade is hot!

SUPTI Yes—hands can be cut off!

The EMPRESS shudders.

She convulses! Cut her head off now!

DAGAROO shakes his head violently.

MIM Extreme love! The eunuch has extreme love for the Empress! I'll split your bones!

HE *is about to strike* DAGAROO *when* NEETO *prevents him. To*
NEETO:

By instinct—you betray us!

NEETO   Because I am able to think! We are here because of her
eunuch! Shall I cut her head off!

SUPTI   Cut her head off!

EMPRESS   *(Speaking in her sleep)* Its roots thick as a man's arm its
roots are livid color it has no seed and is of no use . . . but the
flowers from out its head are worked into wreaths for the gods
and the juice is swallowed. *(*SHE *breathes slowly and deeply)*

SUPTI   *Cut her head off!*

NEETO   Her head full of opium dreams . . . *(*HE *touches her lips)* Her
lips are like a sucking child's . . .

DAGAROO   *(Throws himself down; his voice is hollow and ugly like
a deaf-mute's)* Rotting China . . . the center part . . . the old
woman . . . with wool stockings . . .

SUPTI and MIM   *(Together) Kill her! Kill her! Kill her!*

NEETO   There is sweat on her eyelids like rain . . . drops. The
Empress must not die yet . . . touch the base of her skull
. . . there is opium life there . . . it must be . . . saved.

SUPTI *grabs the hatchet and kills* NEETO.

EMPRESS   *(Still speaking in her opium sleep)* Reason . . . the two
shadows hold in their coldness fire perpetual and downward into
wind . . . these things rest.

Lights go out. THEY *leave.* BOK *enters.*

BOK   *(His voice is a child's voice, high-pitched)* Pi chi lam mim shen sad mem mum *(Laughs)* I do not envy anymore . . . Lan! I do not envy Lan anymore. Lan the acrobat! The shadowboxer! The magician! I have found his weakness . . . it is under the black hair between his legs . . . I can make him cry too. The Empress, she who is my false stepmother, completely loves her own real son . . . Lan—and I hate him. . . . Because I'm alone and very sad and have no real mother, I hate my brother Lan who is only half . . . of a brother . . . we touch each other in the dark . . . we sweat . . . our hands sticky from each other's wetness. . . .

Lights come up.

I will call the future ten thousand years master! I will get the bastard out like a roach from a crack in the wall! *Lan! Lan!* Come to me, your brother! Let's play a game! O Lan—I have some wicked pictures from Pekin—that my own father brought to me! Let's play a game! *Let's play a game! Let's play a game!*

LAN *appears.*

LAN   Where are the pictures?

BOK   Here they are. *(HE shows the pictures to LAN)* See the big round breasts of the woman! Her pink feet! Like little crabs!

LAN   I see you . . .

THEY *stare at each other.* PRINCESS LING *enters.* LAN *and* BOK *dance around her. At first* SHE *is pleased and* THEY *are all lighthearted . . . but a malignant tension happens . . . and* THEY *stop dancing.* LAN *changes the expression of his face to an imitation of* BOK*'s face.*

Does my face look like Bok's face?

PRINCESS LING   Bok's face has more feeling than your face.

LAN Do you like to share . . . the things in this world?

PRINCESS LING *(Happy, playful.* SHE *does not feel or see his intense but restrained anger)* Never! I take it all!

LAN I shall succeed to the throne of China! My reign shall perpetuate the light of China!

PRINCESS LING *(Laughs)* And you are an acrobat and a magician! And I do not know what you want! I do not know what you want to share. Tell me what you want! What do you want?

LAN *(Strange, quiet)* I want Bok.

PRINCESS LING Why . . . why!

LAN Because he's wonderfully made.

PRINCESS LING *(Teasing)* He is a man and you are a man.

LAN I will be the Son of Heaven! The ten thousand years master!

PRINCESS LING *(Laughing)* Yes, your majesty! What does your majesty desire?

LAN I desire Bok.

PRINCESS LING *(Laughing)* That is make-believe! He is a man and you are a man.

LAN Am I or am I not soon to be the ten thousand years master!

PRINCESS LING *(Bowing, coy)* Yes, your majesty!

LAN *(Sinister)* Am I or am I not soon to be the ten thousand years master!

PRINCESS LING *(Humble)* This one looking into your face
. . . says that you will soon be the ten thousand years master.

LAN *(HE does a sleight-of-hand trick)* All below heaven I will rule!
Everything! Go—*you ugly thing! You ugly thing!*

PRINCESS LING I am like water yielding to everyone and everything
. . . the duck . . . the ape, the owl and the tiger. . . . I am a
withered tree. . . . I am fifteen years old . . . and I see the
impurities under heaven . . . mystery of mysteries in a human
. . . Lan who wants to hold Bok as if he were a girl! Their eyes
are one and their ears are one and their noses are one . . . their
mouths are one . . . the wind carries the pollen away. . . . I want
to fall asleep . . . I want to dance while sleeping . . . then things
will change . . . all will obtain goodness . . . if only humans
. . . if only humans could do no wrong! . . . Illusions . . . and
jutting rocks . . . they are dangerous! *(Singing)* I draw water, I
carry fuel. What a miracle, this!

Lights go out. When they come up again a MALE DANCER *is
performing a sword dance.* DAGAROO *is there.* HE *makes guttural
sounds.* SUPTI *and* MIM *speak to the audience. The* EMPRESS
. . . *still sleeps.*

MIM Time . . . endless progression and what is the explanation?

SUPTI Eternity. . . . *She will be!*

MIM She was . . . and as with her soul so with the soul of all. We
are rooted in the natural principle under which each of us lives!

SUPTI She will be divine nature! Shall we cut her head off?

MIM and SUPTI *(Chanting)* Kill her! Kill her!

The DANCER *chops the* EMPRESS's *head off. The* HEAD *rolls.*
SUPTI *picks it up and holds it out to the audience.*

SUPTI   The soul peers out of the eyes, the realm of the intellect.
. . . The eyes are physical extensions, they see heaven and earth.
. . . They plunge downward . . . they plunge from heaven
downward. . . . Punishment justly overtakes the wicked . . . it
is the order of the cosmos. . . . *(Smiles)* The hag . . . the Empress!
. . . was too feeble to lift her eyes toward the higher virtues! Evil
came from her self-will!

HEAD OF THE EMPRESS   But when the body perishes . . . the life
principle remains. No! No! Not . . . life . . . it is the image of
the first shining! Imagine that beyond the heavens there is the
shining sphere!

DAGAROO *screams.* MIM *and* SUPTI *prostrate themselves before
the* HEAD.

MIM   Utterances! As the rays of the sun throwing light!

SUPTI   The gods are divinely speaking to us! And from the head!
(Laughs) Here we have something good—and by our violence!
The reflections of the water are seen . . . but the river is not!

DAGAROO   *Lan! Lan! Lan!*

HEAD OF THE EMPRESS   What could bring to a being anything which
it now does not possess!

DAGAROO   *(Goes to the* HEAD *and opens the mouth wide, speaking
into it)* Lan! Lan! Lan!

HEAD OF THE EMPRESS   The beginning is born from me—it will not
decay. From the fullness of my head the dragons come. To the
line beginning the earth's shadow. Lan's eyes open the way to
things written, remain in one place and never moving.

SUPTI   Will Lan deceive us with his magic? How are we to know
whether to beware, to pray, or to wait!

MIM   Who cannot deceive will not be deceived.

DAGAROO   *(Screams into the mouth of the* HEAD, *chanting)* Yat tsoo chin ma see wong—Lan! Lan! Lan!

> *Lights go down. When they come up three* MONKS *are there, and* LAN, *who lies in a fetal position.* HE *has just been born out of the mouth of the* HEAD OF THE EMPRESS. *His voice combines with the chanting and the musical instruments. Cymbals, etc.*

LAN   I will be saved and I will save. I will be freed and I will free. I will be wounded and I will wound. I will be begotten and I will beget. I will hear and I will be heard. I will be known. I who am all spirit. I will be washed and I will wash.

FENG   Who are you?

LAN   A worm, a moth, a fish, a bird, a lion, a boar, a snake, a tiger, a man.

FENG   Who are you?

LAN   I am you!

FENG   Do you know that you are only a part of yourself? Gain knowledge of yourself. Two are only parts of you. Leap into thyself!

LAN   I go in the end to the beginning.

FENG   *(Intense)* Will you overcome China's enemies!

LAN   Take the stone which is called Draconites from the dragon's head. And if the stone be drawn out from him alive it is good against all poisons, and he that bears it in his left arm shall overcome all his enemies.

FENG   Sharp wits! Sharp wits!

FENG *goes off and then comes back with a dragon.* HE, *with the help of the other two* MONKS, *cuts a stone out of the head of the dragon and places it in* LAN's *arm.*

Who are you? Who are you?

LAN *(Screams)* What is become of me—I cannot see!

FENG Who are you!

LAN *(His voice is strange, distorted)* I am a demon with the likeness of a man but without a head!

FENG Who are you!

LAN I am a demon!

FENG Which?

LAN I am envy. I eat heads, for I seek a head for myself. I have not consumed enough, and I desire a head like thine. What is become of me? *(Screams)* Treachery! I cannot see!

FENG Tell me how you can see!

LAN Through my feelings!

FENG How can you speak without a head?

LAN I am a voice myself! I have obtained the voices of thousands of men! I broke the heads of the dumb on the eighth day after their birth. I can seize and cut off a man's head like a hatchet slash and I put it on myself! *(*HE *screams, convulses, and then lies still)* In me is a female spirit . . . her body is dark . . . her eyes green and shining and her limbs invisible. Her name is Tsu-Hesee . . . she strangles children. *(Screams)* Do not lash me! Li li li li Na na Annnn!

FENG *(To the* MONKS*)* He is released from his body like a god! *(To* LAN*)* Take breath from the rays of the torch! *(*HE *holds a torch to* LAN*'s mouth)* Breathe three times as deeply as you can and you will see yourself crossing over to the heights . . . the mystery is the torch in whose flames the God appears to the gaze of the believer!

LAN *(Screams)* In me is a female! Hanged was I and yet not hanged. Blood flowed from me and yet did not flow. Understand this riddle! Know me then as the praise of wisdom, the wound of wisdom, the transfixing of wisdom, the blood of wisdom, the hanging of wisdom, the suffering of wisdom, the impaling of wisdom, the death of wisdom. *(Chants in a soft voice)* The female in me is abundantly ornamented. I am an open blossom with many rings of petals . . . the petals are points of flame! Heaven and earth had one form . . . the essence was mixed . . . but then the bodies separated and the cosmos took on the whole order that is visible in it. Heaven and earth were one form! *(Screams)* But I bear light! But I bear light—wherein there is not darkness!

FENG What shall you do? Disclose your secrets, reveal the works of the God in you.

LAN Stand round me!

The MONKS *gather around him.*

Respond to me and praise the God with me. I praise the God for the emanation of all treasures. *(Chanting)* Then must I sing! Thus will I leap into love! From love into knowledge! From knowledge into joy! From joy beyond all human knowledge! From knowledge into joy! From joy beyond all human senses!

Drums beat, wine is passed around, chanting turns to heavy sensual breathing.

(To FENG*)* I am the wheat of the Buddha! Thou art I and I am

thou! When thou seest what I do, keep my mysteries silent . . .

LAN *and* FENG *stare at each other, then* LAN *goes to* FENG *and embraces him.* THEY *moan and breathe in ecstasy.*

MONKS *(Chanting)* Now life, now spirit, now door, now way, now bread, now seed, now life, now truth, now faith, now grace. So it is for men.

SCENE 2

A street clash, NON-CHRISTIAN *Chinese battle the* CHRISTIANS. *Huge posters are carried showing the image of the* EMPEROR LAN; *also posters with slogans written, of course, in Chinese. A sign in English, or perhaps a banner, is brought on stage; it says:* China does not want Christianity believing her own religions sufficient for her needs. *The* CHRISTIAN *group is led by two fat* AMERICAN POLITICIANS *who scream out both Chinese and English words. The music combines American marching band with Chinese. People are running back and forth. The incredible noise and frenzy dissipate until finally the voices of the* AMERICANS *are heard.* THEY *are trying to maintain order.*

KLINGER Nee-mong! Attention! Nee-mong! Attention! If a hair on my head is harmed by the non-Christian pigs, and dogs—America will demand and receive a huge indemnity and territorial concessions as well!

GRABHARDT Yes! Yes! T'sang ku yen kung!

LI HANG The religion—the socket of your eye! Speaks of peace on earth and goodwill toward humans! Comes armed for territorial aggression!

KLINGER We're here to civilize you.

GRABHARDT Wu tsung pu Yes! And cut off your pigtails!

The NON-CHRISTIANS *become excited.* THEY *pass among themselves weapons, small sticks and stones.*

KANG   Rise up Chinese! Overthrow the Dynasty! Force out the Americans! The barbarians! The guilty ones! For every crime there is a punishment!

The CROWD *yells:* "Sa ng chut swee ng luk bot!" *The* CHRISTIANS *suddenly pull out huge scissors from their clothes.* THEY *run after and catch the* NON-CHRISTIANS, *cutting off their pigtails.*

KLINGER   We cut off your pigtails and then—then we translate—*you* into American! We translate you into American! *(Laughing wildly)* Translate you into American like a Latin prayer—or a glass of beer!

KLINGER *and* GRABHARDT *are surrounded by the* NON-CHRISTIANS.

Again I say if a hair is pulled out from my head—even one! The Emperor of China will avenge me! The ten thousand years master will avenge me—we are here because of your Emperor!

GRABHARDT   Nee-mong! Nee-mong! The Emperor will cut off your heathen monkey heads—if you touch one little hair on our heads! The Emperor of China is our friend! *(Laughs)*

KANG   You have defiled us! Chang tsu tung yu fan kuo! You cut off our hair!

KLINGER   Tao shuo ai! Yes! Be glad that your pigtails are gone! You monkey faggots! You monkey faggots!

The CHRISTIANS *scream:* "You monkey faggots." *The* NON-CHRISTIANS *chant and the chanting merges with the screams of the other group.*

LI HANG   *(His presence and extraordinary look cause everyone to quiet down.* HE *wears a mask which has no features, just a gaping and bleeding mouth)* I gaze on the past . . . and on the future. I have delved deep, meditating the fate of the Chinese. To what profit are those who have no thought of goodness? How owe allegiance to those devoid of virtue? Hsien kai pa. . . . The stream of time pours . . . everything away. Pour away the strange and perverse beliefs of the foreigners . . . who confuse you with whirlwinds! Obscene flattery! Scissors have cut off your braids . . . they cannot cut out your sorrows . . . in your hearts! O Chinese, would that we could be brothers for all ages! In a life to come! *(*HE *collapses)*

KLINGER   *(Screaming to the* NON-CHRISTIANS*)* Lift your chief monkey up! Ride him on your shoulders! I'm sick of your faces—I'm sick of your faces! Put that monkey on your backs!

THEY *lift* LI HANG *up.* HE *is unconscious.*

Now we go—we all go to pay our respects to the Emperor! *(Laughs)* The need for new tricks is stirring around in his brain. Are we—Americans!—to be blamed because your Emperor wants to learn new tricks! Are we to be blamed because the cut-off head of the Empress still rules China!

HE *signals to them. His* GROUP *pulls* LI HANG *away from the* NON-CHRISTIANS *and castrates him. There is much laughter and like a disease it also spreads to the* NON-CHRISTIANS. *Now the mood is joy everywhere and for everybody.*

The Emperor wants to do acrobatics! And shadowboxing! And learn magic from us! Two white barbarians! What can I say—we are able to change bread into beer—I mean into the flesh of a god! And wine into blood! *(Laughs)* Are you ashamed! Your Emperor has committed no crime against the Chinese people! He listens only to the head of his mother! *(Laughs)* And he wants to learn tricks! Tiu tow ta wan ti cheng!

THEY *all scream:* Tiu tow ta wan ti cheng!

The Emperor wants to penetrate deeply, to probe the secrets of the universe! Like a dream! Like a vision! Like a bubble! Like a shadow! Like dew! Like lightning! *(Laughs wildly)* Now, Grabhardt, now!

GRABHARDT *(Waves a pair of scissors as though it were a baton and sings)* We praise Thee, Father, we give thanks to Thee for the light wherein there is no darkness.

EVERYONE *sings this refrain. The stage darkens.* EVERYONE *leaves. Now* PRINCESS LING *and* DAGAROO *are together. . . . The* HEAD OF THE EMPRESS *sits. A caged owl is there . . . and a fire burns.*

PRINCESS LING I love nothing better than Lan! What shall be? What shall be? We are drawing further and further apart . . . yet my desire is increasing . . . and my heart aches! *(Sings)* Waiting for the beautiful one who has not yet come . . . He competes with the sun and moon in brilliance! *(To* DAGAROO*)* Why should I feel danger, Dagaroo? I only seek the good of my adored Lan. But I hate the wantonness of my adored . . . and I hate when his eyes . . . are *strange.*

DAGAROO *(Guttural)* The only one, the lonely one. . . . Know the male . . . cleave to the female.

PRINCESS LING *(*SHE *has not heard him. Her voice is excited)* Lan's eyes are so strangely brilliant! When he looks at me it seems he sees *himself!*

DAGAROO Through him . . . and with him . . . and in him . . . is a female.

PRINCESS LING *(*SHE *has not heard him)* But he does not love me. . . . I want to say to him, take me with you when you go home!

DAGAROO   The flesh . . . so strong smelling . . . so sweet smelling
. . . a sacred offering. *(HE picks up a flute and plays it)*

PRINCESS LING   *(Singing)*

> Ah sun, ah moon . . . there is a man I want. Wong tso
> tang.
> I wish I had never seen him! Ah sun, ah moon. O shad-
> ows.
> There is a man. . . . Better if I had never seen him!
> Ah sun, ah moon . . . Wong tso tang . . . there is a man
> who says no truth. . . . Wong tso tang. . . . I will never forget
> him!
> Ah sun, ah moon. O Father, O Mother . . . why was I born?
> Wong tso tang . . . I love him beyond all *reason.*

> *(For a while* SHE *is quiet . . . then* SHE *speaks to* DAGAROO*)*
> Explain to me . . . things I do not understand . . . about the monk
> Feng and how I want to scream at him. *"What makes you so
> ugly? I am afraid of you! Go away! Go away ugly monk!"*
> Dagaroo, do you know—that Feng wears a large pearl sewn
> inside his robe . . . and his robe is perfumed!

DAGAROO   You have been taught the four acts of virtue . . . but you
are human . . . with jealous eyes! *(HE grimaces, plays the flute
and dances.* HE *screams in a falsetto voice)* Such a noble young
lady is a fit bride for her lord! It is better to hide the chaste soul's
radiance! The world hates a thing too pure—and devils burst
into laughter!

> *Loud laughter is heard. The lights shine on* LAN *and* FENG.
> *When* SHE *sees them, the pathetic girl-creature faints. This
> makes* EVERYBODY *laugh and carry on, mainly* DAGAROO, *who
> dances and shrieks in glee.*

LAN   *(Pouring some wine for* FENG*)* With my whole heart I adore
you! With bells and drums ringing I rejoice in you! With my
whole heart I honor you!

FENG   I shall transport my Lord, my Emperor to the heights of the ideal ruler! The winds of my instruction will purify the land!

LAN   You are wise and I am only a fool . . . who loves new tricks!

FENG   My Lord will not neglect his duties. . . . My Emperor has come to rule over a new age! My Emperor will have the loyalty of the people! Without him the people would certainly fail.

LAN   I am like dust floating in space. . . . I try to keep it secret. How shall I pass my life . . . how hard must I work? I have no ability in managing affairs. I want only to learn new magic tricks—and some nights I do my acrobatics until the sun comes up!

FENG   Many nights I ride on my donkey over the mountains and I think of new poems. . . . Lan, day and night we will rise and sleep together, drink and eat together. When I die I will give you all the poems I wrote. O friend! O Emperor! He who is born from the womb sees only this world; only he who is born out of himself sees the other world! My reason and heart are joined to yours! When you look at me you see your own nature!

LAN   I love you.

FENG   Then lean on my heart.

THEY embrace.

A door am I to thee who knockest at me . . . a way am I to thee who passest!

FENG motions to DAGAROO to awaken PRINCESS LING.

She moves like a cricket from out of a jar. (Laughs) Dagaroo take the liver from the owl.

DAGAROO kills the owl and removes its liver.

Dagaroo, tie the liver up in the scroll. Hang it up near the fire.

DAGAROO *does as* FENG *orders.* FENG *then walks to the hanging liver and stares at it.*

Princess Ling, stand near the fire!

DAGAROO *leads the* PRINCESS *to the fire.* FENG *writes on a piece of paper and throws it into the fire.* HE *speaks to the* PRINCESS.

I look at you with anger . . . as if you were my enemy. Are you afraid of me?

PRINCESS LING   Yes.

FENG   Do you envy me?

PRINCESS LING   No.

FENG   Do you envy me?

PRINCESS LING   I am afraid!

FENG   Do you envy me?

PRINCESS LING   I am afraid!

FENG   Do you envy me?

PRINCESS LING   Yes!

FENG   Are you troubled by envy?

PRINCESS LING   Yes!

FENG   Ask me to forgive you.

PRINCESS LING   (SHE *kneels before him)* Forgive me.

FENG   You will sleep. And you will see in a dream that you have made a mistake . . . and that you must come to me to make amends . . . otherwise you will feel that you will die. And if you go away, and cannot come to me . . . I will know that you have repented when the liver takes the shape of a crescent, and then the spell will be removed. This I will do by making the sacred letters, and placing them in water, until the writing disappears. I will remember to think that I forgive you.

DAGAROO *leads her to a resting place.* SHE *falls asleep.* FENG *speaks to* LAN.

This that I have done is the secret that is called the treasure of learning. Lan, you will go with me to the length and breadth of all knowledge! My Lord and King, I have grasped and shown you my magic! And through my magic you will set forth the model ways of the Emperors! I give you my heart beyond all worldly ends. My Emperor! Swear an oath that never will anything be allowed to separate us.

LAN   I swear to heaven that I will not forsake you!

FENG   *(Calling to* DAGAROO*)* Tzu ming chieh nan tai lo!

DAGAROO *brings him the opium.* FENG *points to the* HEAD OF THE EMPRESS.

Seek her from out yourself and learn that it is she who takes possession of everything in you—her God, her spirit, her understanding, her soul, her body—and learn whence came sorrow and gladness, and hate and love, and the unwished-for wakefulness and the unwished-for drowsiness, and the unwished-for anger and the unwished-for . . . love. And when you think upon these things, you will find *her* within yourself . . . the one and the many . . . for it is from her, the old Buddha, that you have your beginning.

HE *rises and begins to dance and chant.* LAN *watches him as if*

FENG *was a snake.* HE *joins him in the dance.* DAGAROO *breathes as though his breath were the instrument that moved them to dance. A loud vibrating hum seems to come from the* HEAD OF THE EMPRESS. *The* HEAD *speaks.*

HEAD OF THE EMPRESS Eating the flesh . . . sleeping . . . sleeping on the skins. Look—it is in your heart!

LAN *and* FENG *exit.* DAGAROO *and* PRINCESS LING *remain. The lights go down. The hum from the* HEAD OF THE EMPRESS *becomes very loud. When the lights come up, there is a huge* HEAD OF THE EMPRESS. *The tongue hangs out. Next to the head are the war buttocks: huge buttocks set on muscular short legs. From the opening of the buttocks many different kinds of weapons are thrown out: a shield, lance, sword, bows, arrows, guns, dynamite, grenades, all kinds of old and new weapons.* SOLDIERS *emerge from the hole, screaming and chanting.*

We are dependent on that condition where air, water and oil, where cosh and tanh flow in a droplet . . . it is mixed homogeneously . . . this is the life one is interested in . . . by conviction we make war! Yet means the great thickness earth. In a steady state reaches temperatures of metal. Yet means the great thickness earth! As it must of course be the gray gas. We are dependent on that condition . . . where air, water and oil, where cosh and tanh flow in a droplet. It is mixed homogeneously. This is the life one is interested in. By conviction . . . we make war! In a steady state reaches temperatures of metal. Our skulls heat up!

The SOLDIERS *fight, wound and kill each other with stylized gestures.* DAGAROO *cracks cymbals together like a madman and the* SOLDIERS *scream in pain.*

I am hangwoman, Tsu-Hesee. I eat the brains and lungs of people.

SOLDIER *brains another; another* SOLDIER *stabs someone else.*

I use the roots of men for medicine . . . I breathe into their wounds!

SOLDIERS *lie down in front of the* HEAD *and the* HEAD *breathes on them.*

My tongue drives food into men. I exhale air into men. I pass to them death. My mouth says War! War! War! I war on men! My mouth says split bones! Split bones! I want to eat the bone marrow! Bone marrow! I want to crack the base of skulls! Skulls! Skulls! Scatter bones! Scatter bones! Scatter bones! I do not bury! I do not bury! I breathe incense! I breathe incense! Who ought to rule? Who ought to rule? Corpse eyes! Corpse eyes! The raw feast! The raw feast!

SOLDIERS *hack at each other; bodies are spread all over.*

Cheng, ba na look see kai tsa ut! Come here! You who like the places and times in which duplicity and trickery are done, come here! You who try to deceive those who see things, that they may appear to see what they do not, and that they may hear what they hear not, and that their senses may be tricked! And that they may see what is not true! Bread into flesh! Water into wine! *Agla! Agla! Agla!*

GRABHARDT *and* KLINGER *are marched out.* THEY *are bruised and covered with oil. Slogans have been stuck on their bodies.*

Let their eyes be darkened! That they see not!

A SOLDIER *stabs* KLINGER *and* GRABHARDT *in the eyes.*

And make them shake and sleep the sleep of death!

GRABHARDT *and* KLINGER *are killed. The dead are removed. The lights shine on* PRINCESS LING. *The* HEAD *speaks again:*

The bright moon comes to shine on you, and a man is missed.

Princess Ling! The God of Poetry smiles on you. Look, there are actors, musicians; are they human or supernatural beings! Are they demons!

SHADOWY FIGURES *enter.*

Look, a cluttered landscape with a stream and a bridge, pines and weeping willows, mountain peaks and mist. The genie, Ming Ying Wang . . . is he Lan! The divinity of mountains and streams! He comes in majesty!

LAN *and* FENG *enter.*

Princess Ling, you will be beautiful lying next to Lan . . . your white skin next to his brown. And he will be nude to the waist . . . and he will wear heavy necklaces . . . and a scarf will cross his breast from the left shoulder.

FENG *garbs* LAN *accordingly.*

Then he takes his wand; with this he calls up the ghosts! Gives or takes away sleep . . . and unseals the eyes in death. O you young girl who can weave silk—so much your love and heart!

LAN *goes to* PRINCESS LING *who pretends to sleep.*

LAN How can you sleep? How can you sleep? I have the jewel that fulfills desires! Hsien chung jen.

PRINCESS LING I dreamt of you planting a green bamboo, and I dreamt of a bird that soared over the highest mountain! Tsai chao kuan.

LAN *(HE kisses her cheek)* Laughing eyes! Laughing eyes! I rode on a painted chariot . . . my beloved rode on a horse . . . when shall we become true lovers?

SHE *sighs deeply.*

You sigh . . . like the sound of a fanning wing of a bird. Sigh again. . . .

SHE *sighs.*

Sigh again . . . sigh again . . . and again. No end, no end . . . to your little sighs . . . there is a truth in them. Your heart expresses a single desire, a secret that you never say.

PRINCESS LING   It is bitter to lie in bed alone.

LAN   And again you sigh. Won't you ever stop? No end . . . no end . . . like a million stars in the sky. Is it bitter to lie in bed alone?

PRINCESS LING   Yes, yes!

LAN *looks away from her.*

What are you thinking?

LAN   Something fills my thoughts . . . far away. Once I had a friend who shared my . . . feelings. We walked hand in hand.

PRINCESS LING   Bok?

LAN   Bok. *(HE kisses her)* When shall we become true lovers? *(Again* HE *kisses her . . . and then* HE *draws away from her)* Dien ku shih! You like to kiss!

PRINCESS LING   Shua, hsi . . .

LAN   Yes, I can feel you like to kiss! You would like me to kiss you again . . . you would like to feel . . . pleasures . . . delights . . . of our flesh . . . rubbing together. To nao teng! *(Singing)* To whom shall I send the flowers I have plucked? The one who fills my thoughts has gone afar. We parted from each other though our hearts are one. *(Subtle)* You like to kiss . . . you like

to kiss . . . you like to kiss. . . . With what passion your heart
is burning!

PRINCESS LING   *(Embraces his feet)* Husun hsin! I am sick for love!

HE *moves out of her grasp. Then jumps over her and laughs
. . . and* SHE *laughs because* HE *laughs!*

LAN   With what passion your heart is burning!

Laughing and leaping over her again and again. At first SHE *is
innocent of the evil happening—*SHE *does not see it and so* SHE
*is playful. But then the mood comes to her, mad and terrifying,
as* HE *leaps over her again and again . . . her breathing is as
desperate as his.*

With what passion your heart is burning! With what passion
your heart is burning! With what passion your heart is burning!

*Lighting wild and mad. Then the lights go out completely. The
jumping and breathing sounds are heard along with the music.
Then quiet. The stage is dark.*

HEAD OF THE EMPRESS   Po fen cheng tzu tai chuai nang show kung
shan tien pao tsu fen wu kao ta ha. Understand the head, chief,
first . . . birds, birds and beasts . . . on all sides fierce, savage,
a rat, a mouse . . . brains, a gourd . . . the head to search to search
to search. . . .

The lights come up. LAN *holds* PRINCESS LING *in his arms.*

LAN   An absolute matter of fact fan mei lao. Really and truly
. . . true chen sha. Only . . . only . . . my eyes bite your slender
neck . . . bird-throated girl . . . the perfect ideal tsang yen fang
kuan . . . is locked in my heart. Two men . . . male and male
. . . one and one . . . the whole . . . quiet . . . quiet . . . in a turn
of the eye . . . brothers of one teacher . . . secure the immortality
and the supernatural powers of the way hsien lien. Delicate

tender girl . . . I hold you in my arms . . . I open your eyes wide
with my fingers . . . and stare into them. I laugh loudly Ha! Jo!
Chi! Ha ha! I yawn also, lovely girl, as if we had just wakened
on a heap of grass . . . with a vague feeling, as if we had been
dreaming and had just awakened from a dream. There is not a
single joint or part of our bodies that does not ache. What do
I say to you? What have you inside you . . . that I am so afraid
of . . . that makes me shake my head violently no! No! . . . to
you . . . your soft little hands that make me cold. The coldness
wants to make my stomach burst! *(Laughs)* You are sleeping
your semi-idiotic sleep! Lao kung yu chia! And there's a mass of
broken stones and brambles in my soul. I would like to beat you
until your skin opened and your flesh was ripped up! You said
I had a cruel heart, but my tears wet the pillow through. You
don't know about it . . . hsia ko leng. How strange you looked
. . . on your back . . . with your legs and arms sticking upwards
. . . how strange! *(Laughs)* Waiting for me to play the man! I
was absolutely contented just to watch you with your head
pressed hard against the wall! In your head is a bag of useless
brains—little nun! I feel toward you as I feel toward a three-
legged toad! *(Laughs)* Jang! Shih! Wen! You told me that I am
beautiful! You told me that you felt as if desire were a tiger
eating you! *(Laughs)* When you looked at me. . . . You should
hide yourself on a hilly road in a place where the grass grows
thick . . . and wait there for animals to tung wang kon! And you
tell me that in me is concealed a strange and terrible mystery.
. . . They are just waves and surges in me— *(Laughs)* the
beginnings of the need to do my acrobatics! *(Laughs)* Or practice my magic to open up the tombs of the dead Emperors of
China! *(Laughs)* You tell me that you burn for me! Hsien fu!
Mao li! Your reason is in error! One is all and through it is all
and by it is all and if you have not all! All! So lien tao! Do not
burn for me . . . Tsua ta yang erb. Give sighs . . . take mouthfuls
of breath! You want to want endlessly like an incense burner
burns without end. How you want to grasp! Grasp! Chen kung
shen! Wet me wet me with your femaleness leak out ooze on
me . . . your face purplish while you clutch me! Your love is hard
little clutches which twist my soul—not my soul—my *intestines*

into an icy lump! Your lust has the smell of earthworms coming
out of wet ground. My body shrinks when it touches yours
. . . your rotting body . . . your rotting female part that spreads
out . . . like a crab in the sun! *(HE leaves her and goes to the wall,
leaning against it and breathing heavily)* Think that I think it
strange for a man and a woman to make love together . . .
because they are so different . . . like the wind is different from
a shorn lamb . . . like dew is different from lightning! Hard will
be crushed . . . the sharp will be blunted! Endure disgrace and
become a valley for the world. Going far way . . . means return-
ing. I want to concentrate my breath . . . to make it soft like that
of a little child . . . fan chieh kai yen. In his rule of the Empire,
the sage wishes to make himself like a small child!

FENG *appears.* THEY *stare at each other. When* THEY *speak to
each other, it is as a kind of ritual.*

FENG   That which at birth is so is what is called nature.

LAN   Hsiu sang . . . wash me.

FENG   That which at birth is so to be called nature just as white is
called white . . . teng cho yan.

LAN   Wash me.

FENG   The white of a white feather is like the white of white snow
. . . pao yan.

LAN   Wash me.

FENG   The white of white snow is like the white of white jade
. . . lia tao.

LAN   Wash me.

FENG   *(Intense)* Is the nature of a dog hsing? Like the nature of an
ox?

LAN   Chaun . . . no.

FENG   Is the nature of an ox like the nature of a man? Nan son tien?

LAN   Chaun . . . no.

FENG   *(Washes* LAN*'s body)* The nature of a man is like water. Open a passage for it to the East and it will flow to the East, open a passage for it to the West and it will flow to the West. That which at birth is so, is what is called nature. The nature may be made to be good, or may be made to be evil. Therefore under Kings Wen and Wu the people loved what was good, whereas under Kings Yu and Li the people loved what was cruel.

LAN   *(Intense)* I—I want . . .

FENG   The sage wishes to be a small child! The king fulfills the ideals of government. He who fulfills both is worthy to be the culmination of the world!

LAN   I hate the world.

FENG   If you oppose it, it will make your heart bleed! You are the Emperor! You must not break your vow to me!

LAN   What do you want?

FENG   You must care about your power as the Emperor!

LAN   You will not understand me! *(*HE *grabs up a lute and in a frenzy begins to play it and sing)* You're a thing! Chu chan tui! You hound! Wa yen shang! You're a liar! Kan ta chan! You useless image! Yen shang! You sheephead! Yan chi kan! You son of an ape! Tson kan chien! You imp of Satan! Lien chih tai! Go to hell! Yen tsai chao! You silly fool! Chi mang chiu! Hun tan!

LAN *throws the lute to the floor and then wildly does his acrobatics.* HE *collapses on the floor laughing. The* HEAD OF THE EMPRESS *laughs also.*

HEAD OF THE EMPRESS   His soul is free of earth and heaven. He enters into freedom clutching his buttocks and laughing loudly! Hsun hsin tang sai! He is full of blood and breath! Enlightenment! Like a bird and a beast!

Blackout. Lights come up. PRINCESS LING *is with* DAGAROO. SHE *plays a game of counting her fingers.* SHE *asks a question and while doing so counts each word with a different finger.*

PRINCESS LING   Che li pa. *(Counting her fingers)* Did Lan think my lips were beautiful? Shua hsia. . . . Did Lan want to love me? Kuai hun. . . . Did Lan see how smooth my skin is? *(Monotone)* I am virgin . . . praiseworthy . . . what is the sound that fills my ears? . . . between water . . . and air.

Intense light shines on the HEAD OF THE EMPRESS.

HEAD OF THE EMPRESS   *Sheng tsu hu!*

PRINCESS LING   Sheng tsu hu . . . the ruddy flesh bright! Greater than what follows . . . passes to the lips . . . causes darkness. With what passion my heart is burning. Lai hua chiao tsu erh pan sheng. *(*SHE *takes a burning torch from the wall and holds it to her breast)*

INTERLUDE

LAN *is with* MIM, SUPTI, MONKS, DAGAROO *and* FENG.

LAN   *(Points to* FENG*)* He demanded of me answers! My hair will change color first! *(Laughs)* Thirsty, I will drink wine! Hungry, I will eat!

FENG   I was always by his side—he would always call for me! I found great mysteries which to him seemed wonderful!

LAN   One wind resembles another! He made me vomit excessively!

FENG   I was his tutor!

LAN   Where is the man who taught me to play the lute! If I find him I will be content if my rice bowl is empty! *(Sings)* I think of you whom I cannot see . . . I think of you hun lao shu kuo . . .

FENG   I taught him alchemy! How the gold compound has three parts of its water—the silver compound nine parts!

LAN   He teaches putrefaction! He makes a thing dark and thick, makes it bubble and settle—and putrefy!

FENG   I made shining colors!

LAN   You made earpicks! Nien hsin ching! *(Laughs)*

FENG   I taught him that some processes do not have a physical explanation!

LAN   Like a mountain of boiled rice! *(Laughs)*

FENG   I told you many things, my Master! About stones, alabaster! Things that have no beginning or end! About serpents! Dragons!

LAN   Feng knows how to skin things—how to take the flesh and bones apart and how to reunite them!

DAGAROO *makes guttural sounds.*

FENG   It is celestial virtue!

LAN   A pig!

FENG   *Chu!*

LAN   He wanted me to grow whiskers! For lechery!—At night he
would rip the seams of my robes! He wanted us to be one
hermaphrodite body watered by the dew of heaven! —So I sing
wildly until the moon shines! *(Laughs)*

FENG   He makes no sense because of a chemical—swirling in his
brains!

LAN   *(Introspective)* I sigh my heart away. I will beg . . . until my
body becomes slime and ashes. In my boyhood I was happy
. . . just to see partridges fly . . . and to imitate my mother
. . . paint on widely spaced eyebrows . . . I even made wings and
attached them to my ankles. I would like to begin again . . . to
be filled with the purest blood!

FENG   He is mad! Witless! And I cannot help him—unless he be
induced to perform what he had before promised!

LAN   *(Introspective)* I wish I had crab-shell-green eyes . . . or could
look into eyes of that color. *(To* FENG*)* If you can change the
color of my eyes to green, I will grow whiskers for you—for your
lechery!

DAGAROO *laughs.*

FENG   Liar! Liar!

DAGAROO   Liar Liar!

LAN   *(Rocking back and forth)* Kuo cho fei mi ro she nien shell!

FENG   He is tortured and burned by the spirit of disobedience!

LAN   Dog eyes! Dog eyes!

FENG   There is now only one possibility . . . the spirit must be chained down in hell!

LAN   Dog eyes! Dog eyes! Dog eyes! Change the color of my eyes to green and I will grow whiskers—for your lust! Hsia Tzu!

DAGAROO   Hsia Tzu!

LAN   *(Leaps at* FENG, *screams)* Dragon! Scorpion! Dragon!

MIM *and* SUPTI *pull him away from* FENG.

FENG   He has an internal fever!

LAN   *(Shrieking in a female voice)* I swear to heaven I will not forsake you! I will be with you forever like disease in the bladder! Jen shua niang! Come here Come here come here satisfy me! Suck! Suck! Suck! Sadi sadi agla agla agla wan hsia yao! Feng said, "Heaven is enduring! Suck! Earth long-living! Suck! We shall be twin birds that fly together! I show you my undying love! Suck! Suck! Suck!"

FENG   His is the heart of an idiot! A shrike-tongued barbarian dangerous to the Dynasty! He despises knowledge and would destroy it—and he knows not why!

LAN   *(High-voiced)* Even a clod of earth does not miss the way! Suck! Suck! Suck!

FENG   He moves and grasps and talks like a demon!

LAN   *(Screeching)* Sleep with me under the same coverlet! Walk with me in the sunlight! Write poems for me! Both of us will wear robes made of flowers! We will run after gods and goblins together! Let us smell the plum blossoms of spring together! It is better to hide the chaste soul's radiance! The world hates a thing too pure! When night comes it wets the skin burning with red flowers. Pick them up, petal by petal—neither heaven nor earth can help you!

FENG   *(Monotone)* Rain, sunshine, heat, cold, wind, when these come fully and in order, plants will be rich and luxuriant. If there is extreme excess in any one of them, disaster follows! If there is extreme deficiency in any one of them, disaster follows! Favorable indications are: gravity of the Sovereign, it will be followed by seasonable rain; his regularity will be followed by seasonable sunshine; his intelligence by seasonable heat; his deliberation by seasonable cold; and his wisdom by seasonable wind. The unfavorable indications are . . . *madness* of the Sovereign, followed by steady rain; his insolence by steady sunshine; his idleness by steady heat; his haste by steady cold and his ignorance by steady winds. Thus the actions of the Sovereign, if extreme or improper, exert an influence upon the natural seasons, so that history becomes a divine comedy!

LAN   And what will the Sovereign do in spring, summer, autumn and winter? What will he do! *(Laughs)* Will he produce wood and bone like the wind? Pardon those who have sinned? Repair canals? Repair rooms and gutters? Make compromises of resentments! Open communication between the four quarters of the world! *(Singing)* The soft wind and sweet rain will come, common people will live to a great age and animals will flourish— lan ye hsiao na erh kan mei!

FENG   You like to talk—chiao chien!—of strange theories and to indulge in curious propositions—they cannot satisfy real needs! You are an eternal liar! You are useless! Your spittings could not serve as systematic regulations for government! You deceive and confuse the people!

LAN   *(Falsetto)* Love all things—the universe is one!

FENG   You deceive with your phrases! You betray!

THE WINTER REPERTORY : 216

LAN The universe came into being with me together! Why is your nose always covered with a hard scab no thicker than a fly's wing! Feng! Remember the wise words, the ancient saying: Be humble, you will be made whole—and without any blemish!

FENG Cheng tsan tzu!

LAN On this earth how many are happy?

FENG Kun tsung!

LAN *(Mocking tears)* Happiness is lighter than a feather . . . but no one knows how to carry it . . . calamity is heavier than the earth . . . but no one knows how to avoid it. I suffer great disaster because I have a body!

FENG When you have no body . . . what disaster can there be?

FENG *signals to the* MONKS *and* DAGAROO; THEY *throw a huge cloth bag over* LAN *and drag him away.*

SCENE 3

LAN *is imprisoned.* DAGAROO *is with him.*

LAN First, I put my hands on her—shou meng haou! I'll show you.

DAGAROO *goes to* LAN.

I make my arms hard against her softness . . . she sighs. Her love for me is my weapon. The feeling ceases . . . in me . . . and her feelings increase . . . her skin under my fingers feels like blood not yet dry . . . a star on fire! And I feel wrath in me . . . and melancholy . . . and ice against my teeth and also . . . a tiny joy. If I said to her what was inside me . . . the words would be . . . I will punch you . . . to pulpwood! *(Laughs)* The sounds I would make would be the screams of a vulture against her throat.

Her mouth and legs . . . are open . . . but my mind is working. *(Laughs)* It's heaven's will, shua hsi! In my mind I smear the mucus from my nose on her breasts . . . and drop ants into her two mouths. *(Laughs)* I fill up all her orifices—I'm very generous. *(Laughs)* And she calls me the divinity of mountains and streams and I think of how it would be to urinate on her! She calls herself happy and blessed and how she feels privileged to love me and protect me so that I will never feel lonely or frightened again! And I'm thinking how it would be to throw her into a pig-trough—the pig-slop squashing under her buttocks and her breasts jiggling like rabbits! She burnt her breasts off . . . she sacrificed herself for me . . . and it was an impure sacrifice . . . dirtied by her passion . . . and she was anxious to be a . . . sacrifice! She sustained her purity! Her breast-burning was in accord with her . . . emergency . . . but I am different . . . selfless . . . with few desires. *(Laughs)* She said to me, "Soft weakness overcomes hard strength. A whirlwind does not last a whole day, pelting rain does not last a whole morning." She is like a little sage—a nun! Everything she desired was given to her by me! *(Laughs)* I made her brim over like a dark pool . . . with my tricks—my magic! But she kept her eyes always always on my belly, it seemed to me as if she expected nightingales to fly out of my belly! *(Laughs)* And I told her stories! Stories that I felt she must hear! I wandered along with her in her mind at my own sweet will! While I wandered with her I minced her into meatballs! *(Laughs)* One evening we were looking at a book together, with erotic drawings. I pointed to a drawing, then looked into her eyes and said, "Do people do such things? It's so violent!" Her eyes became wet like the eyes of a goose as she looked at me . . . I even think I smelled her heat! *(Laughs)* And then I told her that I was a virgin! *(Laughs)* And how I would like to know a woman who would teach me a thousand ways to make love! Her mouth opened and she flicked her tongue over her lips . . . and she looked as if she would die! I told her that I would search high and low, continually praying—that I might meet some woman! *(Laughs)* And then she said that I might not have to look very far! She asked me if I had ever made love with a man, and I told her no, how the thought of making love with a man or a woman made me afraid and anyway that I was a magician and an acrobat and had always felt that that was enough for me! *(Laughs)* And then I told her again how I would like to find a woman and learn a thousand ways to make us whirl in the infinitely lovely storm of sweet feeling! And I held her— and I trembled against her soft body—like this! I trembled! *(LAN holds DAGAROO to his chest)* She was like a flower dropping petals before my eyes or a mouse with its intestines hanging out. *(Laughs)* "Ti lu fu kan chi tsan;" she said and I said, "Tsan fen huan wah." She said I was a perfect male! A man! I felt her wanting . . . to seize me, grab and scratch and tickle me. I called her . . . my pepper seed . . . my pip . . . my kernel of love . . . and inside my head was an axe and I was cutting off her head! *(Laughs)* She tried to straddle me! She grew fur and feathers before my eyes! Her feet changed to hooves! I touched her shining hair . . . and in my head I was touching pigs' bristles! I kissed her lips . . . and the lower half of my body . . . vomited! I called her . . . my little chicken and she called me her rooster! Her cock-bird!

Whistle blows.

What is that?

DAGAROO   The pigeons.

LAN   *(Introspective)* The melancholy wailing of the whistles carried by the pigeons . . . they are wheeling in midair! It reminds me of the souls of the dead roaming about in space seeking for a resting place.

DAGAROO   The pigeons carry news about the war.

LAN   *(Reciting)*

You suffered starvation in deserted villages
Always you saw ahead of you a gutter death,
And yet you were incessantly singing

Of the glorious events that occurred each day.
Soldiers died, lay wounded on battlefields;
Stars fell down the sky,
A thousand horses vanished in clouds.
To all these your life was a sacrifice.
Your poverty still glitters and shines
Like the rags of a deceased saint,
And the least tatter that remains
Is endowed with magic powers.
Their crowns and purples in this light
Are shoddy when compared to yours.

DAGAROO   You are the Emperor! And you are a prisoner!

LAN   I do not feel shame because of detention in prison . . . and it
is no disgrace to be insulted. To desire few things is an inner
cultivation. *(Pause)* I would have aggression stopped and pro-
pose disarmament!—The nation has suffered terrible wounds
long enough. I laugh at the folly!

Whistle blows.

Strange birds . . . they reach the corners of the earth . . . If only
I lived in a different place . . . in a forest of peach trees! It would
be so fragrant . . . I could preserve my moment of life. See my
eyes, they're filling with tears. . . . I have no magic to overcome
death. . . . Give me some wine.

DAGAROO *pours him wine.*

A fire burnt down a beautiful cottage . . . long ago. The boy who
lived in the cottage went to live in a boat . . . far away . . . one
glance from him . . . embraced the heavens! His spirit was always
calm . . . I want to get drunk! I would love nothing better than
to get drunk. Red beans grow in the south . . . I love nothing
better than red beans . . . Bok . . . where is my brother Bok
. . . far away . . . one glance from him embraced the heavens
. . . red beans . . . I would gather them in great quantities for

I love nothing better . . . than . . . I wonder if he's a drunkard . . . or a murderer . . . his bright hungry tiger's eyes . . . his jacket of purple . . . his fingers making patterns on the green moss . . .

DAGAROO He has a sword and a spear!

LAN He has a sword and a spear! We were twin birds . . . our skinny legs intertwined . . . dead . . . won't the sorrow ever come to an end! Won't the sorrow ever come to an end! We pressed our wet bodies together . . . yang ta fan . . . I knelt down and saw his nails gleam silver . . . I put my palms on his chest . . . tau pan shen . . . when we kissed our mouths turned into leaping fish! He put his feet around my neck . . . I crushed him with my hold . . . my sweat dropped on him . . . I licked it off his beautiful eyelids . . . lia hu chi, his body quivered under me. From the back of his neck, and his navel . . . and the small of his back . . . he howled with love. Two lovers! Two lovers! The moon in bed with us! He is lost . . . I cannot find . . .

Whistles blow.

Why don't pigeons sing? Why don't pigeons sing! Why don't pigeons sing!

Whistles blow.

O . . . but I know there is much more than war in this country! Where does this young girl come from who keeps staring at
me?

DAGAROO *laughs.*

Who is she who keeps peering at me in a sneaking way? (LAN *picks up some dirt and throws it into his own face.* HE *rubs the dirt away, looks around, searching)* I am astonished! She has gone away! If we meet again—she would not recognize me for my face is covered with dirt! We are as far away from each other as liver and gall. . . . She has rolled away from me like a muddy egg. Hsiao yen chu hun!

DAGAROO *and* LAN *laugh; then* DAGAROO *begins to puff air out of his lips.* LAN *watches him, an excitement builds up in both of them.* THEY *stare at each other.*

Love all things, the universe is one. The egg has hair. Ying contains the whole world. A dog may be a sheep. The horse has eggs. The frog has a tail. Mountains produce mouths. Tortoises are longer than snakes. A white dog is black. A married woman has a beard. A fowl has three legs. Fire is not hot. Wheels do not touch the ground. Eyes do not see. Things never come to an end.

Lights alter into strange shapes. LAN *begins to spit out what appear to be little animals.*

INTERLUDE

PRINCESS LING *appears. Her skin sweats blood.* SHE *begins to pray to the* HEAD OF THE EMPRESS. SHE *is burning with ecstasy and reaches out to* LAN. SHE *screams in a shrill vibrating voice as Arab women do during celebrations.* LAN *gestures magnificently, then plunges a golden dart into her.* DAGAROO *is emotionless.* HE *watches her die, then* HE *leaves and returns with a female puppet, elaborately dressed.* LAN *approaches the puppet reverently.* LAN *strips the clothes from the puppet and garbs himself with them. There is intensity and an undercurrent of violence in his gestures.* HE *makes up his face and puts on the puppet's wig. Sometimes* HE *speaks in Chinese:* Chia tang erh chieh chung tso ting hung ko sao ti kung chi yang mon chia ya tzu fen chieh tsung keng pien hang te chung nao kua yen hisn. *The words may be said in any order. The actor uses the Chinese tonal sounds; he is guided by his mood and his own inspiration.* DAGAROO *emits his guttural sounds or says the word* Hu! *After* LAN *is finished dressing,* HE *is transformed into a woman.* HE *walks and moves gracefully and naturally.* HE *does not parody*—HE *is a woman while* HE *is dressed in women's clothes.* HE *carries on a dialogue with the new herself, changing his voice to a female tone when* HE *speaks as* SHE.

LAN SHE What has the power of the Emperor to do with the spontaneous changes of all things? We follow two courses at once. There is nothing which is not the "that," another thing's other; there is nothing which is not the "this," its own self. Things do not know that they are another's "that"; they only know that they are "this." The *that* and the *this* are alternately producing one another!

LAN HE The *this* is also *that!* The *that* is also *this!* The *that* has a system of right and wrong.

LAN SHE The *this* also has a system of right and wrong.

LAN HE Is there really a distinction between *that* and *this?*

LAN SHE There is nothing better than to use the light of understanding! *(Laughs)*

LAN HE *(Laughs)* The light of reason!

LAN SHE Following two courses at once. *(Laughs)* I have the love of life!

LAN HE How do you know that it is not a delusion? How do you know that you are not dreaming?

LAN SHE *(Laughs)* Because I pervade myself! I am a duality! I am 10,000 things also!

LAN HE I am the blending of two breaths! Heaven and earth!

LAN SHE I pray that you do not die!

LAN HE Bathed in the sun, washed in the moon, among the hundred precious things I grew.

LAN SHE Are you a flower?

LAN HE Yes! *(Laughs)* And I give off an evil odor—like a roomful of chickens!

LAN SHE Be quiet! I am thinking of lying naked in a green wood. O, why have I returned?

LAN HE Because you heard the squeaking of flutes! And you saw my footprints!

LAN SHE But I shall not follow you! Because I have just drunk a glass of wine. And I do not know what will come.

LAN HE I will make sandals of hemp. Will you twist the threads for me?

LAN SHE Yes! If we sit together in the candlelight!

LAN HE I love to think about that! And your little feet white as frost! And your new dress is an endless bright shining!

LAN SHE O Emperor—I tremble because of your love! I tremble like a silkworm on a leaf! I remember when no man wanted to live with me.

LAN HE Tender girl, you are a moon of shining flowers!

HE *dances and chants. The stage is darkened.* SOLDIERS *appear;* THEY *speak in Chinese; voices overlap.* THEY *laugh and scream. The mood is bright and happy, then changes to darkness and dread as suddenly as a weather change, and as unpredictably.* SOME *of them yell insults at* LAN. HE *screams back at them in his female voice.*

LAN SHE   You are lumps! Foolish lumps! Tsung king hsin! Lumps with mouths! Depraved! Depraved! Depraved! Hsing! Tu! Kua!

A SOLDIER *runs to* LAN *and prostrates himself before him, breathing heavily.*

Lin so yang. We are like leaves. When a leaf falls off a branch and rots there is nothing left of it. Ti chan how—death in the world. I will make a new world! I will make new people and animals! Yen chu hun—all sorrow will end—will flow away! *(Laughs)* Your dethroned King is a mere woman—who holds in her hand no murdering sword but a pretty jade comb! *(*HE *takes out a comb)* My only woe is that I might lose it in my overflowing jewel box *(Laughs)* or that it might be broken in two by a rough soldier— *(*HE *is introspective, recites a poem)*

He said he was a fool.
He beat his breast.
He bit his fingers.
He bent over and let men kick him in the ass.
He smiled.
He giggled.
Some men giggled with him.
He heard them giggling.
He was remorseful.
He was last.
He knew when he had had enough.

(Responds again to the SOLDIERS*)* —or that it might be broken in two by a rough soldier—who would thump me in the dark—no, no, the daylight! Like a wild animal! *(*HE *begins to mince slightly. Then stops and confronts them all)* Hu chi shih shih! I'm easy to understand! I'm yielding! I'm humble! I can hum! I can chirp! Look! Sheng tsu! I am no Emperor! No tyrannical fierce King! I am not dangerous! Grab me by the nape of my neck! Spread out my buttocks! I can be penetrated through by you, by all of you! I am no Emperor! I am no Emperor!

IMAMU AMIRI BARAKA (LEROI JONES) is a poet, playwright, essayist, and currently spiritual leader of the Committee for a Unified NewARK, as well as a prime mover in Newark's Spirit House Theatre. He has taught at the New School for Social Research, Columbia University, the University of Buffalo and San Francisco State College. His major plays include *Dutchman, The Baptism, The Slave, The Toilet,* and *Slave Ship*—seminal works, along with his recently published *Four Black Revolutionary Plays,* in the creation of the black theater movement in America. In addition to writing plays, he has published many volumes of poetry *(Black Magic Poetry; In Our Terribleness),* prose *(The System of Dante's Hell; Raise Rays Race Raze: Essays Since 1965),* musicology *(Blues People; Black Music;* and the forthcoming *Life and Times of John Coltrane),* and anthologies of contemporary black writing, most recently co-editing *Black Fire* with Larry Neal. A recipient of John Hay Whitney and Guggenheim fellowships, he is a member of the International Coordinating Committee of the Congress of African Peoples.

JULIE BOVASSO, born in Brooklyn and a pioneer of the Off-Broadway movement, is the recipient of four *Village Voice* "Obie" Awards for her ventures in playwriting, acting and directing, as well as one given at the first Obie Award Ceremony in 1956 for founding "The Best Experimental Theater in New York." This was the Tempo Playhouse where she was instrumental in introducing the works of Genet, Ionesco, and Michel de Ghelderode to this country. She has made memorable acting appearances in *The Maids,* Jack Richardson's *Gallows Humor,* and most recently as Said's Mother in the Chelsea Theater Center's marathon production of Genet's *The Screens.* She also appeared at La MaMa in her own *Gloria and Esperanza,* for which she received a triple Obie—as playwright, director, and actress. Her other plays include *The Moon Dreamers, Monday on the Way to Mercury Island,* and

Down by the River Where Waterlilies Are Disfigured Every Day. A 1971 Guggenheim Fellow, Miss Bovasso teaches drama at Sarah Lawrence College and the New School for Social Research. *Schubert's Last Serenade* was first produced at La MaMa E.T.C. in July, 1971, directed by the author and designed by James Hardy and Rachel Park.

ED BULLINS teaches playwriting at the New Lafayette Theater in Harlem, of which he is an Associate Director. A highly vocal leader of the emerging generation of black playwrights, he is a Guggenheim Fellow and winner of the Vernon Rice and Obie Awards, the latter for *The Fabulous Miss Marie*, which recently appeared in *Scripts* magazine. His other published work includes *Five Plays; The Duplex: A Black Love Fable; Four Dynamite Plays;* and a volume of short stories, *The Hungered Ones*. In addition, he has edited a paperback anthology, *New Plays from the Black Theater*, and is editor of *Black Theater* magazine, published by the New Lafayette, where most of his plays have had their premiere productions. His productions at other New York theaters include the American Place Theater performances of *The Electronic Nigger* and *The Pig Pen* and Lincoln Center Repertory's controversial restaging of *The Duplex. Dialect Determinism* was first performed at the Firehouse Repertory Theater, San Francisco, in August, 1965, directed by Robert Hartman and designed by Louie Gelwicks and Peter Rounds.

WILLIAM M. HOFFMAN, born in New York City, majored in Latin at the City College of New York. He has worked as a poet and librettist-lyricist as well as playwright, and has edited three anthologies of new American plays. Seven of his plays have been produced at various Off-Off Broadway theaters, including *Thank You, Miss Victoria*, which was later presented Off-Broadway in *6 from La MaMa*, directed by Tom O'Horgan. He has worked at the Playwrights Unit, the McDowell Colony, lectured at the Eugene O'Neill Foundation, and his plays and poems appear in many anthologies of new American writing, the most recent being *Saturday Night at the Movies* in the forthcoming *Off-Off Broadway Book.* He writes: "I am currently *making* plays, using improvisational techniques of my own design to create theater pieces, with a group of actors called Wolf Company, which has presented four plays of mine, including *Nut Bread,* and also with teenagers in the Lincoln Center Students Program. I grow plants, play ping-pong— and bake bread." *A Quick Nut Bread to Make Your Mouth Water* was first presented by Wolf Company at Norman Hartman's Old Reliable Theater Tavern in July, 1970, directed by the author and designed by Charles Terrel and David Adams.

ADRIENNE KENNEDY, born in Pittsburgh and raised in Cleveland, attended Ohio State University, but found the social structure there so opposed to black people that she did hardly any academic work and started writing at the age of 20. Her writing began to receive real recognition in 1962, when she joined Edward Albee's workshop, and in 1964 her *Funnyhouse of a Negro* received the Obie as Most Distinguished Off-Broadway Play of the year. Her other plays, which have appeared in many anthologies, include *A Lesson in Dead Language, A Rat's Mass, The Owl Answers,* and *A Beast Story,* the last two having been presented at the New York Public Theater under the title *Cities in Bezique.* As a Guggenheim Fellow, she spent a year in England, where the National Theatre performed her adaptation of John Lennon's *In His Own Write* and *Sun* was commissioned by the English Stage Company. She is currently working on a dance scenario for Alvin Ailey, and on an opera libretto. *Sun* was first presented by the English Stage Company at the Royal Court Theatre, London, August, 1969, directed by Nicholas Wright.

LEONARD MELFI holds the record for the number of plays produced at Cafe LaMaMa—thirteen, since 1962, the most recent being *Cinque*. In addition, he has had plays produced on and Off-Broadway and on television, and has written several screenplays, the most recent being *Lady Liberty*, starring Sophia Loren. His Broadway productions include *Night*, in the triple bill *Morning, Noon and Night*, and the sketch "Jack and Jill," in the revue *Oh! Calcutta!* Six of his plays are collected in a volume called *Encounters*, and one, *Birdbath*, is included in *Best Short Plays of the World Theatre*. His plays have been translated and performed in six European languages and Japanese, and he has just completed his first novel, *The End of Marriage Forever*. *Cinque* was first performed by La MaMa Troupe at the Royal Court Theatre, London, in March, 1970, directed by Wilford Leach. It was first performed in New York by the Actors Experimental Unit in May, 1971, directed by Jules Aaron.

MEGAN TERRY was a founding member of the Open Theatre and worked extensively with their playwrights' workshop, out of which emerged her celebrated and precedent-breaking *Viet Rock*, which ran for some time Off-Broadway and has been performed by many theaters throughout the world. Among her other significant works are the short plays *Calm Down Mother* and *Keep Tightly Closed in a Cool, Dry Place*, both originally performed by the Open Theatre; *Massachusetts Trust*, staged by Tom O'Horgan for La MaMa Troupe; *The People Versus Ranchman*, an Off-Broadway success; and the Obie-winning *Approaching Simone*, a tribute to Simone Weil. Several of Miss Terry's works are collected in *Viet Rock and Other Plays*, and a number appear in Samuel French acting editions. She has completed a musical on the Frankenstein story, and is currently writing a play about Don Juan as a woman. *Sanibel and Captiva* was first performed on WGBH radio in Boston, as a winner in their contest for new radio dramas.

ROCHELLE OWENS is the author of many innovative and controversial plays, of which the best-known is *Futz*, an Obie-winning play, first directed by Tom O'Horgan, which has been performed throughout the world, as well as being made into a feature-length film. It is the first of five plays in her published collection *Futz and What Came After*, which also includes the memorable *Beclch*, a source of some uproar when it was first staged by Andre Gregory at Philadelphia's Theatre of the Living Arts. Among her recent plays are *He Wants Shih!*, *Kontraption*, which recently appeared in *Scripts* magazine; and a musical, *The Karl Marx Play*, which is included in *The Best Short Plays 1971*. Miss Owens has been a Guggenheim Fellow and spent a year as an ABC Fellow in Film Writing at the Yale School of Drama. In addition to her plays, she has published four volumes of poetry. Her poems first appeared, in the early 1960's, in LeRoi Jones' magazine *Yugen*, and her most recent collection is *I Am the Babe of Joseph Stalin's Daughter*. She has given numerous poetry readings, as well as recording her adaptations of primitive and archaic world poems. She is a founding member of the New York Theatre Strategy and the Women's Theatre Council, and lives in New York with her husband, the poet George Economou.